Time management for manic mums

Get control of your life in seven weeks

Allison Mitchell

HAY HOUSE

HAY HOUSE
Australia • Canada • Hong Kong
South Africa • United Kingdom • United States

First published and distributed in the United Kingdom by:
Hay House UK Ltd, 292B Kensal Rd, London W10 5BE. Tel.: (44) 20 8962 1230; Fax: (44) 20 8962 1239. www.hayhouse.co.uk

Published and distributed in the United States of America by:
Hay House, Inc., PO Box 5100, Carlsbad, CA 92018-5100. Tel.: (1) 760 431 7695 or (800) 654 5126; Fax (1) 760 431 6948 or (800) 650 5115. www.hayhouse.com

Published and distributed in Australia by:
Hay House Australia Ltd, 18/36 Ralph St, Alexandria NSW 2015. Tel.: (61) 2 9669 4299; Fax: (61) 2 9669 4144. www.hayhouse.com.au

Published and distributed in the Republic of South Africa by:
Hay House SA (Pty), Ltd, PO Box 990, Witkoppen 2068.
Tel./Fax: (27) 11 706 6612. orders@psdprom.co.za

Published and distributed in India by:
Hay House Publishers India, Muskaan Complex, Plot No. 3, B-2, Vasant Kunj, New Delhi – 110 070. Tel.: (91) 11 41761620; Fax: (91) 11 41761630. www.hayhouse.co.in

Distributed in Canada by:
Raincoast, 9050 Shaughnessy St, Vancouver, BC V6P 6E5. Tel.: (1) 604 323 7100; Fax: (1) 604 323 2600

A catalogue record for this book is available from the British Library.

ISBN 978-1-4019-1563-6

Design: Leanne Siu

Printed and bound in Great Britain by TJ International, Padstow, Cornwall.

Time management for manic mums

Dedication

This book is dedicated to all mums. In particular, my own mum who is one of the truly marvellous variety, also my dad, and of course the apples and blueberries of my eye, Chris, Hannah, Callum and Laura.

Acknowledgements

My thanks to everybody who has supported me in my most manic of motherhood moments. I'd especially like to thank a few people who have been particularly supportive whilst I was writing this book: Clare, Jackie, Lou, Kathleen, Debby, Belinda, Louise, Rachel. Paul for his coaching. An extra special thanks goes to Wonderbird Lou Gimson. And of course to all at Hay House.

Contents

Foreword

Dear Allison,

As I sit here watching the late-night omnibus edition of Coronation Street, sipping a large glass of Baileys, thinking about the dishes piled high in the sink, my unplucked eyebrows and the school trip letter needing my signature, I decided to write to you and ask for your help.

You see, my life has become a mish-mash of things to do, all jumbled and colliding into one another. The tasks I am expected to complete as a working mother with three daughters seem completely overwhelming. I just never have the time to do it all, let alone enjoy any of it. The events of today really got me thinking that I need help to create more time. This is how my day began:

This morning I had an appointment at the gynaecologist's clinic for a colposcopy following a bad smear test result. I'd been up three times in the night with Natalie's nightmares, so when my alarm sounded I pressed the snooze button twice. I now didn't know if I'd get there on time. I quickly dressed, shoved the children into my next-door neighbour's house, jumped in the car and drove too quickly down the road, doing up my seat belt as I went. Then it dawned on me: I hadn't left enough time to go to the cashpoint. I only had £1.60 in my purse. Not enough to pay for the hospital parking! Inspired, I decided to park up a side street and catch the bus. Unfortunately, as I waited at the traffic lights the Number 26 flew round the corner and passed me at great speed in the bus lane. Like a cross between Ayrton Senna and Evel Knievel, I spent the next 20 minutes playing 'beat the bus'. I lost.

As a last resort I abandoned the car in my dentist's car park and walked the rest of the way to the hospital. Did I say walk? With a ten-minute journey ahead and my appointment in seven, I ran! When I arrived I was delighted to find that I hadn't unpacked my handbag from the children's picnic last week and I was able to salvage a couple of almost-dried-out baby wipes. I popped to the Ladies to clean myself up. Whilst locked in the loo I heard my name being called and rushed out, leaving my handbag and car keys in the cubicle. I bravely underwent the 'procedure', which lasted 20 minutes. It certainly gave a whole new meaning to the term 'go for the burn'! As I sat with my legs in the air, I thought to myself, 'What a sad tale: the only time I haven't rushed today was whilst clamped in a rather unflattering position to a gynaecologist's examination table.'

The last time I found myself in this position was when I gave birth, which is when my 'loss of time' first began. It's also when I stopped dedicating time to looking after myself.

When I was pregnant, I made sure I ate, exercised and rested properly. I wanted to do the best I could for my unborn babies whilst I was sharing my body with them. What about now they're here? I can't remember the last time I had any 'me' time in the past 14 years.

Please help me to find some elusive time for myself and to run my life in an organized and calm manner, instead of the pulse-racing, manic way I live it today.

Yours hopefully,
A Manic Mum

Dear Manic Mum,

I write in response to your request for more time and a calmer life. I know you'll be delighted to hear that what you want is perfectly possible to achieve. Believe me, I speak from personal experience. People are sometimes surprised to learn that I, too, used to live my life in the same manic way that you do. That is, until I learned the secrets to getting more time. These secrets lie in the Seven Truths of Time Management. Apply these Truths to your life and your problems will be solved. I receive so many letters like yours that I now find it difficult to keep up with them. So I thought it would be useful to write the secrets and Truths down, so you can discover them for yourself, then pass them on to others. I look forward to hearing how you get on.

With warmest wishes,
Allison

Introduction

How to Find Time to Read This Book!

If you have no time then it does rather beg the question, 'How will I find time to read this book?!' Believe me, with three children and a busy life myself, I fully understand the challenge.

I've written the book with this in mind. And what better place to start than with some tips and suggestions for getting this book under your belt, and its help and advice into your brain and life, in just seven weeks.

Halve Your Reading Time

Unfortunately for me, I had to write this epic one word at a time. You, however, can read it two words at a time, immediately halving your reading time. Not bad. Try it out. It's easy to read two words at once. When reading silently to yourself, don't say the words out loud in your head. This will really slow you down. Look at them, take them in without saying them, then move on. When you get used to reading two words at a time like this, try it with three and four.

Use your finger to point at the words. Pull it along the line so your eyes have to work a little quicker than usual to keep up with your finger. I know pointing at words is what you do with your five-year-old, but it really does work. Go on, have a go, try it now. Before you know it you'll be such a proficient speed-reader all you'll have to do is hold the book against your head, and its contents will enter your brain by osmosis.

Time-chunking

Just as you'd eat an apple, a pear or an elephant one bite at a time, devour this book one chunk at a time. Break it down into a series of manageable pieces. It's already broken into seven chapters. Each chapter can be read over the course of a week.

Set aside 15 minutes a day for reading. Make a time when you'll be able to do it. Maybe bedtime, on your lunch break or waiting to pick up from school. Finding time to read a whole book is tricky. Finding time to read for 15 minutes a day, that's achievable.

Planning

At the end of each chapter I give a rough estimate of how long the exercises take so you can plan when to do them.

Enjoy Yourself

Look upon reading this book as a treat. It's for you. Make it something you look forward to each day. Perhaps promise yourself a coffee to read it with, a hot chocolate at bedtime, or combine it with a bubble bath. Make it something that you want to do. Feel free to write in it, make your own notes, personalize it in any way you like!

Reward Yourself

Give yourself a reward at the end of each week. This will help keep you motivated.

Dip In and Out

The book is stuffed full of top tips to help you manage your time. Flick through and pull out any that appeal to you or look particularly helpful. Try a new tip every day. See what a difference it makes.

Read It Back to Front

The book does have a logical sequence, but don't feel obliged to follow it. Make the book work for you. Look at the chapter outlines below. If one of them particularly applies or appeals to you, head for that chapter first and read the others later.

Summary

Week One – What's in Your Egg Timer: Sand or Gold Dust?

Do you know how much your time is worth? If not, turn the page and read on.

Week Two – Where Did All My Time Go and Please Can I Have it Back?

If you have no idea where all your time disappears to, this chapter will help you locate it.

Week Three – How Much Time Do You Want?

If your life has lost direction and you're stuck in a rut, this is a one-stop shop to pick up the life of your dreams.

Week Four – Become the Mistress of Your Own Time

If your disastrous disorganization is wasting your time, get yourself sorted and read this chapter first.

Week Five – Time Management for the Masses

If your family are slowing you down and you feel like you spend most of your time chasing them, this will be compulsive reading.

Week Six – Put Off Procrastination

If you're of a delaying disposition and your favourite word is mañana, don't delay, read this today.

Week Seven – Human Doing to Human Being

If you feel like a hare and you'd rather be a tortoise, rush straight to seven.

Week One

What's in Your Egg Timer: Sand or Gold Dust?

An Ode to Needing More Time

When I gave birth and became a mummy,
I didn't expect a big flabby tummy,
My boobs and my bottom, they've all gone south,
I'm so tired and I've ulcers in my mouth!
And all my time, where has it gone?
Seem to spend most of it wiping kids' bums.
A moment for me?
I've no time to pee,
Got to get Callum and six friends their tea,
My house is a mess,
I'm a mum in distress,
I feel like a failure I have to confess.
The state of your life you have to assess,
When the only chance you get for a rest,
Is to unashamedly strip off your vest,
And sit with a child hanging from your breast,
While worrying if this will lead to arrest.
Feel like I'm stuck in a big black hole,
Which of course would be fine if I were a mole,
But I'm not, and I'm losing my heart and my soul,
Next time I'll think harder 'bout birth control.
People tell me I'm doing fine,
But I don't feel like I'm up on cloud nine,
I just want to know, when will my life be mine?
Answer my prayer, please give me more time.

Time Truths 1 2 3 4 5 6 7

There is no more time

Give Me More Time

We're all mums here, aren't we? So let's be honest: what mother isn't totally shocked by how little time she seems to have? Not only shocked by that, but how her day seems to be gobbled up by the demands of others. I've often heard reports from shell-shocked first-time mothers of their inability to find the time to undertake the most basic of functions during the course of a normal day. I'm thinking, for example, of tasks such as getting themselves dressed, brushing their hair or cleaning their teeth before sunset, by which time of course it's almost not worth bothering anyway.

Whatever age our children are, we've all been there, haven't we, in that place of despair? Stressed and almost on our knees because our lives no longer seem like our own? If you've ever hollered from the top of your voice, 'I need more time!' then you're not alone. This, I'm afraid, is the common lament of millions of mothers around the globe. In a world where having it all, being it all and doing it all seem to be what we're all supposed to want, mums everywhere find themselves stuck in the spin-dryer of life, whizzing around at 100 miles an hour in a confused, bemused and terribly crumpled state.

Whether you've got tots, teens or something in between, your life's probably full to bursting.

Desperate to get it all done, Manic Mums all over the place are crying out for help. We need more time, and not just for the drudge work, either. We want quality time. We want time for us.

Armed with this book, time will no longer be your master. The help on offer here will let you claim back what's rightfully yours: your time.

Tip! Keep a small box stocked with wrapping paper, sticky tape, scissors, labels, etc. so it's always to hand when there's a present to wrap.

The Time-trap of Motherhood

When you have children, your whole concept of time, motion and space changes, doesn't it? Everything takes longer, everybody moves slower and your once-clear house is cluttered. Spontaneity goes out the window, along with your old life. And this, as they say, is just the start of it. As your children grow older, it doesn't get any better. They just make more and different demands on our time. Believe me, I know – my own children are well past the nappies stage. We all love our children to bits, but it has to be said they are incredibly time-consuming, whatever their age.

When I first had my children I was absolutely astounded by how much time they took up. I felt like I was caught in a time trap. Fitting everything in became nigh on impossible. Despite the fact that everybody and his dog had warned me in no uncertain terms exactly what it would be like, I didn't listen. I just didn't believe them. It was not within my realm of comprehension that life could ever be as chaotic – and as out of my hands – as they were suggesting. Let's face it, how difficult could it be to look after one tiny child? Don't they sleep most of the time anyway?

These were my famous last words as an expectant, uninitiated mum, who thought life would be pink, fluffy and easy with a small baby. These thoughts and words were washed away with the flood of my waters, which broke in the fruit and veg aisle of the local supermarket. They were muffled by the voices of the Gods of Providence shouting, 'Wake up and smell the breastmilk, honey!' Then they were well and truly eaten along with a large mouthful of humble pie. I was presented with a dollop of down-to-earth reality from the University of Life. It came in the form of a small, colicky baby with a ferocious set of lungs and an insatiable appetite for mummy milk.

Welcome to the real world of motherhood, where babies don't sleep – and neither do their mothers!

What was even more surprising was that this bundle of joy didn't arrive by stork under the gooseberry bush in my back garden, either. Only after a week in hospital and 24 undignified hours of pushing, shoving, puffing and panting did she appear. Exhausted but undaunted, and clearly elated by the arrival of my new little girl, I mustered the energy to get out a bottle of lukewarm champagne from my maternity bag – I've always been one to pack the essentials and I wanted to celebrate her safe delivery. She was worth all the effort, and I'd been looking forward to this for nine months (I'm talking about the champagne, now!). Along with the bottle I pulled out three glasses: one for my husband, one for the midwife, and one for me. Now, I'm not too posh to push, but I do like to keep my tabletops free of ring marks. So I also pulled out what I thought was a packet of coasters. My mum, bless her, had popped them into my hospital bag a few weeks earlier.

'You'll need these,' she'd said with a wink.

As I gave one to the midwife to place her goblet on, she smiled knowingly. She reliably informed me that, yes, I would be needing these pads, but not to catch stray drips of champagne. No, this was a hulking great pad to shove unceremoniously down my bra, to prevent me from flooding the maternity ward with breastmilk! Surely not, I thought. A couple of days later her prophecy came true. Overnight, my boobs became as large as twin Mount Everests, covered in veins that looked remarkably like an accompanying Himalayan route map for fearless mountain explorers. Not only did I need the pads, but a bra with cups the size of two parachute silks to contain my now out-of-control and greatly expanded breasticles.

What a fiasco.

As it turned out, 'flood' was a real understatement.

Gushing out horizontally at great force, what I produced was more like a tidal wave sufficient to consume a whole town or any person unfortunate enough to be passing within 50 metres. Thank goodness for the super-absorbent 'coasters'. Never had I experienced anything like it before. My life – and my body – were no longer my own.

As the days, weeks and years went on, I came to understand that having children robs you of many things: your dignity, your sleep, your sanity. And the biggest loss of all is measured in seconds, minutes and hours. Seemingly tossed away with the placenta, and all the clothes that used to fit, your time disappears down the plughole along with the new baby's bathwater. You're left holding your increasingly grizzling bundle of joy surrounded by scores of chores, dirty floors and a horribly neglected social life. As you wallow in the depths of despair about the plight of your life, you begin to feel great regret for not having made the most of what you had before you were bestowed with a child, your time.

Time and the Pelvic Floor

Time, if you will excuse the analogy, is a little bit like your pelvic floor. When you had it and it worked perfectly you didn't know what it was, and certainly didn't pay any attention to it or feel particularly grateful for it. But when you lose control of something this important, suddenly you know all about it. I'm sure most of you mums out there know exactly where your pelvic floor is now, and it's nowhere near your feet (well, unless you had a really traumatic labour). I discovered that this small muscle was really quite important to have in perfect working order. Oh, the forgotten joy of being able to sneeze or laugh without the need to wear a sanitary towel the size of a large duvet. Oh, to be able to jump up and down without fear of your tampon falling out. Time is the same, you just never knew how lucky you were before it stopped being fully available to you and you lost control of it.

Tip! *Keep a mini writing kit with stamps in your handbag.*

Doting Dads, Dishevelled Mums

When a new father arrives home after what he considers a hard day at work (and to be fair you also considered it a hard day until you had looking after Junior to compare it to) he is confused by what greets him in the sitting room. Has his wife slipped into her negligee in anticipation of an early night of passion, or is she still really in her nightdress from this morning? A quick sight of the crusty milk stains on her left sleeve and the wet patch close to her now 'out of bounds' cleavage gives the game away. Has that cup of cold coffee with scum on top really been there since breakfast? This poor woman has barely had time to take a drink and get dressed. She's lost the plot. She's out of control.

How did this happen? I mean, how time-consuming can it be looking after a baby? Well, of course he finds out when Mum finally gets nipper off the breast, makes a break for freedom and spends a night out with the girls.

In the settling dust left by a mum on the run, Dad is left holding the baby, bottle and wet wipes. After an evening running the gauntlet of dirty nappies, feeding, winding and walking up and down the same few feet of floorspace with a crying infant, and consulting extensively with his mother on the phone about what on earth he should be doing, he joins the rest of us in the real world. Yes, he too discovers that childcare is amazingly time-consuming.

And as most of you know, it doesn't get any easier. When children start school the demands on your time change, with after-school activities, homework, friends, camps, swimming galas, parties, revision, sleepovers and the like, and life in the home with older children can have the complexity of a major military operation.

Colin Powell himself would gasp at the manoeuvres required to maintain the smooth running of an average household with older children. Whatever age your children, the truth remains: there just never seem to be enough hours in the day to get it all done. And it's no wonder when we take a look at the job description:

Mum Wanted

Wanted, caring person with great interpersonal skills and lots of energy as personal assistant, mentor, trainer, nurturer, cook, cleaner, personal shopper, social organizer and bottom-wiper for small helpless creatures. The ideal candidate will have the patience of a saint, skin of a rhinoceros, tongue that can easily be held and amazing time-management skills.
Hours: 24 a day, seven days a week, minimum contract 18 years.
Pay: £0,000,000.
Benefits: car (can be parked guilt free in the mother-and-baby spaces at the supermarket).

Who on earth would willingly apply for this post? Whoops, we all did. I, being particularly crazy, did it three times over. Like you, I want to believe that I'm a sane, vaguely intelligent person. But with millions of others we're rushing around like headless chickens in an attempt to do the job that is being a mum, while still retaining a shred of sanity. Some of us have even got two jobs: 'ExecuMum' by day and 'Manic Mum' by night.

So what do we do? We soldier on and do our best, but often end up feeling hopeless, helpless and worthless. We get paid nothing for doing what can only be described as the most important and demanding job in the world. I don't wish to sound like a sulking teenager, but it has to be said: how unfair is that?

Tip! *Exercise while you watch TV.*

What Value Do You Put on Your Time?

In a nutshell, what lies at the heart of many of our issues is that we just don't feel valued. In a society where financial remuneration is linked with status and respect, mums score pretty low. Nobody values or rewards us financially for what we do.

The message is loud and clear: your time is worth nothing. We receive the message, and as a result we don't value ourselves, what we do, or our time.

I recall vividly after the birth of my daughter, the first time I was asked a question about what I did for a living.

I remember replying, apologetically, that I was 'only' a mum. I hurriedly added that of course I would be going 'back to work' soon. It was as if when I was working in a 'proper' job I was acceptable, but being a mum made me some kind of outcast, a lactating lunatic not worthy of being engaged in intelligent conversation. I was only socially acceptable to other mums.

What about you? When you think about your own life, what value do you put on your time? If you aren't sure, answer the questions below. They'll help you get a handle on the value you place on your time right now.

Something to think about ...	Agree	Disagree	Partly agree
I value my time less now I am a mum.	❑	❑	❑
I let other people take advantage of my time.	❑	❑	❑
If I had to pay myself a salary for the job of being a mum I wouldn't know what to pay.	❑	❑	❑
I'm not doing things that are important to me.	❑	❑	❑
I've never really thought about my time and myself as precious resources.	❑	❑	❑
If I do paid work I feel that this time is more valued.	❑	❑	❑
I feel bad when I think about how I manage my time.	❑	❑	❑
Other people treat my time with less respect now I'm a mum.	❑	❑	❑
I never get everything done that I want to.	❑	❑	❑
If I only had one year to live, I would not carry on spending my time as I do now.	❑	❑	❑

If you've agreed to a lot of these, then chances are you're not valuing your time as much as you could. If you're not valuing your time, my guess is you're not getting as much done in a day as you could. There's a good chance you don't feel at your best right now. If you start valuing your time, you'll automatically start to value yourself and feel better about yourself too. It's a double whammy, a win/win.

Time, the Ultimate Designer Brand

Whatever you do for work, in and out of the house, and whatever age your children, the first step in rectifying your time-management dilemma is to get a sense of how much your time is really worth. Putting a value on your time is essential if you want to get more out of it. You may think that this is a bit of an odd thing to do, but I promise that if you do this you will begin to feel differently about yourself.

To illustrate the point, let me take you back a number of years to just after my daughter was born. I'm going to tell you about my jeans. You may wonder what on earth this has got to do with valuing your time, but stick with me.

I was desperately trying to get my fat rear end and flabby tummy back into my jeans after the birth. Sadly, my propensity always to use the excuse that I was eating for two had led to excessive weight gain – 42 pounds to be exact. This meant to return to my pre-maternity weight, I needed to deliver a 42-pound baby. I gave birth to an eight-pound baby. You do the maths! It only takes a few people to say to you, 'When is the baby due?' when you gave birth four months earlier, for you to get pretty serious about shedding the excess. I went on a diet.

When I finally reached my goal, I left my daughter with my mother and went shopping for a whole day. Wonderful.

When it came to the jeans, there was a huge choice and I wallowed in the almost forgotten luxury of having time to go and look at everything that took my fancy. I even got to try things on without having to wrestle the pushchair into the changing room. One pair I tried on were Calvin Kleins. Whoopee. They were very expensive, more than I would normally spend on jeans, but boy did I want them. I'm sure that they didn't really look better than any of the others. Shallow as I am, I wanted them because they were CKs. I was putting extra value on them. I was prepared to pay more for them than for any of the other jeans.

Everywhere in life you find the phenomenon of perceived value. At the supermarket you pay more in Waitrose than Wal-Mart, in a car showroom more for a VW than a Skoda, and in the jewellers more for a Rolex than a Swatch. Essentially, these things are all the same, it's their perceived value that's different. Because the perceived value is higher, people pay more and treat the item with more respect. After I bought my CK jeans I really looked after them, in a way that I had never looked after any other jeans. For example, I didn't tumble-dry them.

Other jeans I'd have happily tossed in the dryer, blatantly ignoring the care label. When we pay a lot for something, we're more likely to value it and look after it.

Put a Price on Your Head

As mums, because we don't get paid for our time we tend not to value it. And because we don't value it, neither does anybody else. In a recent survey by Norwich Union, the UK's largest insurers, nearly 50 per cent of dads thought it would cost less than £10,000 a year to replace a mum. Some 16 per cent said it would cost less than £5,000. On 'Planet Man', perhaps these figures stack up. How about in the real world? If the average mum had to be replaced it would mean recruiting at least three people, working eight-hour shifts.

What would it be like if you thought differently about your time and put a value on it? What would it be like to think about yourself and your time as a designer brand? Just imagine for a moment that you are paid for the job of being a mum. What would your time be worth? What value would you put on yourself? How would your family cope without you? If you weren't available and you had to be permanently replaced, what would it cost? In 2000 the Office of National Statistics calculated that the value of unpaid housework and informal childcare in the UK was almost £700 billion. That's roughly £30,000 a year per mum. A full-time nanny would command a salary of between £29,863 and £43,805 depending on where you live. On 'Planet Man', only 5 per cent of dads thought it would cost between £30,000 and £50,000 to replace a mum and only 5 per cent thought it would cost more than £50,000. So, what are you worth?

Think about all your unique qualifications, skills and abilities. What would you have to pay to get those? What salary do you deserve? Decide on a figure. It's up to you. The sky's the limit. When you've decided on your salary, work out your hourly rate. The table on the next page gives a rough guide.

Tip! Focus fully on what you are doing if it's important to you.

Annual Salary £	Hourly rate (based on 24 hours 365 days per year)
1,000,000	114
750,000	85
500,000	57
250,000	29
100,000	11
50,000	6
25,000	3
10,000	1

You might think that working out a salary for a job that pays nothing is an odd thing to do. However, unless you can begin to value your own time and give it a sense of worth, it is unlikely you will ever make the most of it. If you think it's worth nothing, your inclination will be to treat it like it's worth nothing. If you believe that your time is worth £1 million a year, do you think you would be living your life like you are right now? Would you be choosing to do different things with your time?

Time is one of the most precious resources we have. Although as a mother you may not be financially rewarded for the work that you do, your time is worth just as much as anyone else's. All the money in the world can't buy one of your precious hours. Your time is priceless. Whatever you value it at now, double it, triple it, quadruple it. Start thinking about yourself as the best designer brand there is.

'Our costliest expenditure is our time.'

THEOPHRASTUS (370–287 BC)

What's in Your Egg Timer: Sand or Gold Dust?

I like to think of the passing of time by picturing a giant egg timer. You know, the ones that have a glass dome at each end.

You turn it upside down and sand passes from the top dome to the bottom one. When the top dome is empty and the bottom one full, your egg is ready. Usually, these timers are filled with sand. I find it's helpful to think of the egg timer of your life being full of something more precious: gold dust.

For a long time I treated my time as if it were sand. Time management is about creating a mindset that values and makes the most of the time we have. Like gold dust, it's precious. At some point it will run out. As sure as the sand in the egg timer filters down to the dome below, so does the gold dust of our lives. We never can be sure just how much of that precious dust remains.

Oh No, There's No More Time!

Yes, I do hate to be the one to disappoint, or indeed be the bearer of bad news. Ladies, the sad reality of our situation is, there is no more time. It is our sombre responsibility to make the most of what we have. Since time began there have only ever been 24 hours in any one day, 168 hours in a week and 8,760 hours in a year, not one more, not one less. It's the most constant fact in this world of chaos and change. With the reassuring regularity with which my husband moans about my shoe collection, day turns to night and night to day. Like a packet of sweets, or a bottle of good wine, you always want more when they're finished. Unfortunately, you can't pop down to your local corner shop and pick some up. You get your ration every day. Use it or lose it. The first of the Seven Truths of Time Management is 'There is no more time'.

How Much Gold Dust Have You Got Left?

Think for a moment. How much time do you really think you've got left on this earth? Fill in the egg timer below. In the bottom dome, draw the gold dust that has

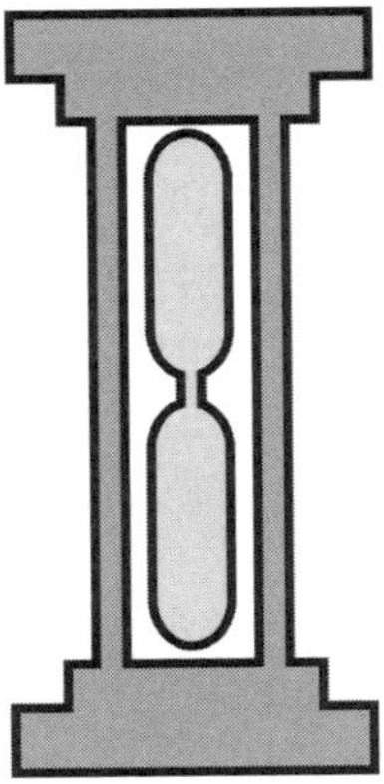

The Egg Timer of Your Life

been used up so far in your life. In the top dome put the dust of your life that remains. I find there's nothing quite like this exercise for focusing the mind on the value of your time.

Tip! *Every now and again, instead of making dinner, make reservations.*

There Is a Silver Lining

OK, I've made my point. There is no more time and the time we have is going to run out. Sorry, folks, I don't want to depress you here, but there's a bit of a trend in the human race and so far, nobody's managed to buck it. We will all eventually expire, kick the bucket, conk out or, to put it bluntly, die. On a more cheery note, in this fog there is a little chink of sunshine. Yes, there is hope. Time is like any other scarce resource. It is possible to learn how to make the most of it. Like money, fuel or good-looking men, those who handle their resources well seem to have more of them. Time's the same. If you treat time like the precious resource it is, value it, respect it and learn how to manage it, suddenly you will seem to have more. What you have will go further. The fact is, you will still have the same amount. It will just seem to you, and others, like you have more. Get the value of time sorted, begin to act as if it's priceless and things will start to change in your life. You will get more done in a day. I promise that you will be living a more fulfilled and happier life. People will look at you and say, 'How do you do it all?' They will want to know your secret. This book will become what a good financial manager would be for your money. Contemplate for a moment this little story about a father and his three daughters.

A Story about the Value of Time

At the turn of the 19th century there lived a great and wealthy engineer. Despite his riches and status in the community, he was a humble man who never forgot his roots. He knew that hard work and shrewd decisions had helped him get to where he was in life. He was keen to ensure that his three daughters had the same values and that they, too, knew how to make the most of the resources that life had to offer. He thought long and hard about how he might achieve this. One day he came up with an idea. He decided that when it came time for them to leave home and be more independent in the world, instead of handing them a fortune on a plate, he would take a different approach. To each child, instead of the share of his fortune they were expecting, he gave a solid lump of steel worth 100 pennies.

They were, unsurprisingly, a little surprised. They'd been expecting hard cash (as children do!) but, as they knew their father well and respected him, they listened to what he had to say.

'To each of you I am giving a precious resource. With all the technologies we have today it will be possible for you to turn this resource into something valuable and to make your own fortunes. I have given you all the same, one equal weight of steel and a ticket to wherever you want to go in the world. Return in a year's time and show me what you have achieved.'

Lauren, the first daughter, decided to stay at home and make horseshoes with her steel. Unfortunately, farming was not the flavour of the day and horseshoes were not much in demand. She did her best, making 105 horseshoes using the old-fashioned manual methods employed by a blacksmith. She sold them at a penny each, making 105 pennies. A 5 per cent return on her investment.

Beth, the second daughter, recognized that she could use technology to her advantage. She went to Sheffield, a centre for excellence in the fashioning and manufacture of steel utensils. She used her metal to make high-quality, razor-sharp knives. She was able to make 300 knives that sold for three pennies each, making her 900 pennies. An 800 per cent return on her investment.

The third daughter, Rose, went on a mission to find a way of making the maximum amount she could from her steel. In Switzerland, great leaps forward had been made in watch-making. The accuracy of timekeeping was very much down to the quality of the internal mechanism of the watch. Seeing this as a golden opportunity, Rose used her steel to make very small, top-quality watch cogs that were in high demand. She sold them for ten pennies each. She made 1,000 cogs, yielding her 10,000 pennies. A 9,900 per cent return on her investment.

At the end of the year, they returned to their father. He was full of praise, for each one had succeeded in making money. He said to them, '*The most precious of all the resources you have in life is your time. Like your piece of steel, you have a set amount, and like your steel, depending on what you do with it, it can yield you more or less. Think, my girls, what do you want to make with your time: horseshoes, knives or watch cogs? The choice is yours, be sure to make the right one.'*

What Are You Making with Your Time?

We have a choice about how we spend our time. We can fritter it away on something that produces lesser results and doesn't give us much in the way of a return.

Alternatively we can spend it on something that pays higher dividends in our life and really reflects our highest values. If we choose to put a high value on our time and decide to spend it on things that matter to us, suddenly our world starts to change. The things we want in our lives start to appear. How do you feel about your life right now? Do you feel like what you are doing reflects the highest values in your life? Or are you frittering away your time on a treadmill, partaking in activities that don't satisfy you? What are you making with your time: horseshoes, knives or watch cogs?

> Tip! *Fill up your car whenever you can – not when you have to. Running on empty can be very stressful.*

What Are You Losing Out on in Your Life?

How are you choosing to spend your time? What are you losing out on by doing things that aren't really of any value to your life? In accountancy, this concept is known as 'opportunity cost'. Buying one thing means you are effectively choosing not to buy something else.

If I go back to my example with the jeans, buying the expensive jeans meant that I chose to miss the opportunity of buying a pair of shoes. If I'd chosen cheaper jeans I'd have had cash left to buy accessories.

It's all about choice. Making one choice means we miss the opportunity to do something else. We live our busy lives making different choices about how we spend our time. On the whole we don't stop to give much thought to what we're spending it on. Consequently, we don't think about what we might be missing out on because of the choices we're making.

From the Mouths of Mums:

'I feel like life is just passing me by really quickly, and I don't seem to be doing anything that's of real importance to me. I know looking after the children is important, but I seem to spend all my hours doing menial chores when really I'd like to be spending more quality time with my children and partner.'

Same Resources, Different Outcomes

Let me introduce you to Manic Martha and Perfect Paula. They've been friends for years.

They went to school together and now live in the same street. Paula and Martha have similarly paid part-time jobs and two children each, aged between two and ten. Their husbands work for the same company and have identical incomes. You'd expect them to live similar lives. Nothing could be further from the truth. Their lives are different because of the choices they make around how to live them. Glimpse into their worlds and see if any of their traits are reflected in your own life. As you contemplate their lot, be curious about their behaviour in relation to how they manage time. What's it gaining for them and what is it costing them?

Tip! *Don't buy knickers with the days of the week on for your children. You just don't want the hassle of trying to persuade a five-year-old to wear Tuesday's knickers on Friday. It wastes minutes (or even hours, depending on how determined your child is!).*

Manic Martha

Manic Martha lives up to her name. Always frantic and on the go, she leaves a trail of destruction behind her. She never has time to clear up from one thing before she's on to the next. She often abandons things halfway through. Her children are always late for school. Other mums are filled with fear if they see her entering the school gates before them. They know it means that they too must be late.

Always full of enthusiasm, Martha is amazingly optimistic about what she will be able to fit into her day. Needless to say, she usually gets to the end of it having achieved barely half of what she set out to. Too many things happened to stop her, not that she really had any meaningful plan of action to begin with. Much to the frustration of her family, she's always late home from work.

When you call her and tell her that you are in the area and would love to pop in for a cup of coffee, she's delighted. The sudden prospect of an unexpected visitor will have her hurriedly scurrying round her untidy house to give it a quick once-over. She'll be moving heaps of ironing from public view and haphazardly shoving piles of paper into cupboards. She was supposed to tidy up that morning but instead had to take the dog to the vet when it swallowed a Barbie doll's head, left on the kitchen floor from yesterday.

Manic Martha's always promising herself that one day, when she has time, she will get round to giving her house a good sort-out. She seems to thrive on chaos and often wonders how her friends can be so organized. She spends half her time looking for things that she's lost. She still hasn't unpacked her suitcases from last summer's holiday. Although she's always busy, she never gets anything done. She knows she's lost control of her time, and doesn't know how to get it back.

Perfect Paula

Perfect Paula lives up to her name. She's fun and friendly. When she commits to something, she never lets you down. She always follows through. She's got time for herself and others, too. She truly appreciates the value and scarcity of time, and makes the most of it. She seems to get more done than most in the average day. She's got a stash of secret short-cuts that allow her to get more done than other people. She's able to say 'no' nicely if you ask her to do something that she hasn't got time for. She knows what her own priorities are and sticks to them.

The most organized woman you've ever met, she has a plan for everything. She never seems hurried and gets things done, one at a time, in a highly efficient manner. She does all this despite the fact that she has two children and a rather lazy husband. Her life seems to run like clockwork. Her children are immaculately presented. They never turn up to school with breakfast on their faces or a Pop Tart stuck to their elbow. Even when the children are at home there doesn't seem to be any chaos.

She holds down a responsible job, is calm and organized. She always walks through the door at night on time with a smile on her face. With effortless ease, she achieves the impossible – yes, she is even able to keep the inside of her car clean! Her house looks like the cover of *Homes and Gardens*. She finds time to entertain, go to the gym and play tennis with her friends. She knows where she's going on holiday next year, and seems to have a long-term plan for her life. She's already talking about how she will fund her retirement at the age of 45. Her children seem calm and well adjusted. They do lots of things as a family and seem to get on really well. They are very relaxed and at ease with each other. An inspiration to us all.

Tip! *Before you start something ask yourself 'Is this the best use of my time right now?'*

Are You Manic Martha or Perfect Paula?

I have to admit that before I got to grips with time management I was a Manic Martha and I hated the

Perfect Paulas of this world. I wanted to be the kind of woman who, when she went on holiday, had manicured nails, exfoliated skin and a bikini line waxed to within an inch of its life. As a Manic Martha, my manicure consisted of a quick chop at my nails with the children's craft scissors while I sat on a suitcase bulging with nappies, forcing it shut with my overweight behind (which for once was coming in useful). In the service of multi-tasking I would be simultaneously typing an e-mail to my boss on my Blackberry, using the only free body part available to me, my nose. Having forgotten to book in my bikini wax, my decision regarding hair removal revolved around whether to take a pair of garden shears or a set of rollers to deal with my proliferation of shrub-like growth when I reached my holiday destination. Decisions, decisions.

You'd like to believe that being Wonder Mum is boring and dull. Who really wants to be that straight and organized? Do I really want my car clean on the inside? Surely a little bit of stress is good for you, isn't it? No, the lady doth protest too much. You know that deep down you want a bit of what Paula has. Maybe not drawers with socks ordered by colour, but wouldn't it be nice to have a life with room to breathe, and space to fit in everything that's important to you? Of course it would. The fact that you're reading this book means you must want to move forward with your life and get more time. Whatever your starting point, it doesn't matter. This book will help you make the most of the time you have.

Learn Perfect Paula's Magic

How will you learn the magic spells that Perfect Paula weaves with her time? How, like a piece of elastic, will you be able effortlessly to stretch time? Will it require major surgery or a DNA transplant to transform you into a Time-management Queen? The answer is a resounding 'No'. It really isn't that difficult, nor is it complicated. Believe me when I say if I can learn it, you can learn it.

Everything you need to know is found in the Seven Truths of Time Management. They're not difficult to understand or apply, and they're infinitely more useful than most things you were taught at school. Perfect Paula understands and lives by these Seven Simple Time Truths. One week at a time a new truth will be revealed to you and over the next seven weeks you'll integrate them into your being, as you transform from Manic to Marvellous. You already know the first one, but just to make you salivate, here's a little taste of what's to come:

Time Truth One: There is no more time

Wise up, use what you've learned in this chapter and start valuing your time. You are your own designer brand.

Time Truth Two: To save time you must first know how you spend it

If your time is like gold dust, you don't want to lose any. Like a dripping tap or a leaky pipe, time seeps away unnoticed. Pinpoint your leaks (and we're not talking about your plumbing!). Work out where all your time goes so you can get loads more.

Time Truth Three: Know what you want, then you'll find time to look for it

You know you want more time, but do you really know exactly what you want to do with it? Come on, you mums, dare to dream. If you really had all the time in the world, what would you do? My guess is it wouldn't be making ham sandwiches for Ben and Imogen's packed lunch. Get in touch with your values and rekindle your dreams. Learn how to set goals, not just for the day-to-day things, but all the things that are important to you, your dreams. Start finding time to live them.

Tip! *Stop feeling guilty about all the things you haven't done.*

Time Truth Four: Take control of time or time will take control of you

If you don't become the mistress of your own time, then time will become your master. Learn how to create a powerful but simple planning system which allows you to track and achieve your goals. Take control. Get back in the driving seat of your life.

Time Truth Five: Systems save time

Systemizing your life will save you oodles of time. Develop systems that will help you manage yourself and your family. Your children will love it as you transform from a mum on the run to a mum who's fun.

Time Truth Six: The cost of putting things off is higher than the price of doing them

Getting things done at the right time is the key to successful time management. Learn how to put off procrastination and get everything done on time.

Time Truth Seven: If you can live in the moment you can expand time

When we savour our time, it seems to last longer. Imagine a life where every moment is one of quality. What would that be like for you and your family?

Truth Seven takes you one step beyond pure time management. Learn how to develop a relationship with time. One that allows you to dance in the moment and savour life, like the most delicious tub of Ben and Jerry's ice-cream. Yum! That's it, easy. Each week learn the details of a new truth until you are as organized and as fabulous as Perfect Paula.

Let's start with Truth One. There is no more time, so value what you've got. Try out the exercises below for a week. Get clarity about how much value you place on your limited time.

Tip! *Book your holidays for weeks that include a public holiday, so you use up less allowance.*

Actions for Week One

Each morning as you look in the bathroom mirror, set a positive intent for your day. Promise yourself that you will value your time. Approach your day as if you were being paid for everything you do. (five minutes)

- At the end of the day before you go to sleep, think for a moment. Ask yourself the following questions:
  - In what ways have I valued my time and myself today?
  - In what ways have I not valued my time and myself today?
  - How can I value myself and my time more tomorrow? (five minutes)

- Choose seven of the time-saving tips that appeal to you from the pages of this book. Every day for the next week, try out a new one. See how much time it saves you. How do you feel when you save time? (Ten minutes to peruse tips. It then depends on what you choose, but it should be saving you time anyway.)

Summary

- All mums want more time, but, like your pelvic floor, when you have a child you lose control of it.

- Any mum who reads the job description and still applies is mad. There's no pay and no one (including you) values your time.
- Time is the most precious resource in the world and must be valued. Treat your time like gold dust. Put a value on your time and live up to it.
- Time will run out. By choosing to do the wrong things with your time, you'll lose out in life.
- You can live your life like a Manic Martha or a Perfect Paula. If you choose to be a Manic Martha, it comes with a price tag.
- If you want more time, get to grips with the Seven Truths of Time Management and your life will be transformed.

Now you're ready for Week Two, where we'll be identifying how and where your time leaks away, so you can plug the gaps and start claiming back those hours, minutes and seconds you so desperately need.

Week Two

Where Did All My Time Go and Please Can I Have it Back?

An Ode to Where All My Time Goes

A new day is dawning,
Not surprised that I'm yawning,
Not slept beyond five since motherhood came calling,
It's either the kids or my fat husband's snoring,
One of the two wakes me early each morning.
So I get out of bed,
With my day thrust ahead,
Dressing the kids first, then getting them fed,
At six have a shower,
Feel I've been up for hours,
Why does my day seem so long and so dour?
Perhaps have a coffee,
Put Sam on his potty,
Trying to toilet train's driving me dotty.
At midday, I'm waning,
And I don't like complaining,
But still 14 hours of this dull day remaining,
At the end of the day,
I know I will say,
What did I accomplish today?
It feels like my time's just been frittered away,
I'd just love to know,
As I slug my Bordeaux,
Where on earth does all my time go?

Time Truths 1 2 3 4 5 6 7

To save time you must first know how you spend it

The Champagne Lifestyle

Let's assume that after the insights from Week One and practising how to put more value on your time, you have come to the same conclusion as me: your time really is more on a par with champagne and caviar than fizzy water and dry bread. If you're beginning to think about time in these terms, then you might also want to become a bit more careful about what you do with it. I mean, who wants to waste a drop of good champagne? I certainly don't.

On the whole we are terribly careless with our time and don't treat it with the respect it deserves. We just lose it here, there and everywhere, then wonder why we haven't got any left at the end of the day. Can you imagine if we took that approach with our children? (Tempting though it is.) We know where they are at all times, where we have put them and what they are doing. Not so with our hours!

Benjamin Franklin once said:

'If time be of all things most precious, wasting time must be the greatest prodigality, since lost time is never found again.'

Yes, like the backs of your earrings, once lost time is gone for ever. However hard you look, you can't get it back. Have you ever pondered the fact that your time just seems to disappear without trace? I'm sure you have. If you were to think about how you spend your average day, how would you respond to the statements below?

Something to think about ...	*Agree*	*Disagree*	*Partly agree*
I have no idea where all my time goes.	❑	❑	❑
I am always busy but seem to achieve nothing.	❑	❑	❑
I set out to do lots of things, but they never happen.	❑	❑	❑
I always seem to get distracted and interrupted when I try to complete something.	❑	❑	❑
I feel like my life is slipping away.	❑	❑	❑
Sometimes I feel like I'm on a treadmill (and it's not the type to help you lose weight).	❑	❑	❑
I struggle to remember what I did yesterday.	❑	❑	❑
There seems to be no routine to my day.	❑	❑	❑
Things usually take me longer than I think they will.	❑	❑	❑
One day just seems to run into another.	❑	❑	❑

If you find yourself agreeing or partly agreeing with these statements, then it's time to take stock and find out what plughole your time is going down.

The Importance of Knowing Where Your Precious Resources Are Going

It makes sense really, doesn't it? If you value something you don't want to waste or lose it. Unfortunately, unless you can identify where all your gold dust's going, how can you possibly save it? Time Truth Two clearly states: 'To save time you must first know how you spend it.' You have to be able to account for every minute, every speck of gold dust.

I first came to terms with the concept of saving precious resources in the long, hot summer of 1976. In this year the UK had its hottest summer on record. As a carefree eight-year-old, this was pure joy. The down-side was that as the summer progressed, water became scarce. Eventually it was rationed. One of the results of the shortage was that families were encouraged to find creative ways to save water. My parents, upstanding citizens that they are, always keen to do their bit, got quite carried away in this time of national need. They made me share bath water with my younger brother. Yes, I was subjected to bathing with my smelly sibling, yuck! Suddenly I was praying for rain.

As a fairly resourceful (but mostly determined) child I set myself the task of working out how to oust my brother from the bathtub. I knew the only thing that would wash with my parents was that any suggestion I made had to relate to saving water. So I set out to find a way to make our water go further. Find a way I did.

It was a hot, sticky July evening. My brother and I had taken our mandatory joint bath. My mum was out of the way, putting him into his pyjamas. It was safe to put my master plan into motion. I'd worked out that if I could get a handle on how much water the average bath used, then I could make the suggestion that instead of us sharing a bath, we could have one each, sharing the water between us. For my plan to work I needed to know how much bath water we were using in total. So, armed with a jug, I scooped water out of the bath, and threw it out the bathroom window onto the garden below. One jugful after another I threw, keeping count of the total number. My mother, who has a well-honed sixth sense for suspicious activity, enquired from my brother's room,

'What are you doing, Allison?'

'Oh, nothing,' I replied, sheepishly.

She might have been convinced, if not for the untimely arrival of my father. Unfortunately he'd chosen the moment I threw jug number 24 out of the window to venture outside to read his paper in the evening sun. As you can imagine, for the next five minutes I had some serious explaining to do to a very wet father and equally annoyed mother.

Once my parents got the gist of what I'd been doing, they were somewhat sympathetic, saw the funny side and assisted me in my calculations. For the remainder of the summer we had one bath each. Fifteen jugs of water apiece. Eureka! I'd applied the Second Truth of Time Management to my water problem. To save time you must first know how you spend it. By calculating what I was using I knew how much I had to work with. Only then could I come up with an accurate alternative for how to use my water in a way that suited me better, and got me more of what I wanted.

Tip! *Have a list of phone calls you need to make, then fit them into spare moments.*

Where Are Your Precious Resources Going?

The lamentable truth is that most of us have no idea how the 24 hours we get every day are spent. Where do all yours go? If you want to know, you really do have to stand back and take stock. If you don't know how much you've got and where it's going, how can you expect to get more?

From the Mouths of Mums:

'I have no idea where all my time goes, it just goes.'

Don't be fooled into thinking it's only big tasks that eat away at your time. Very often minutes and seconds can seep away from your life, unnoticed.

They're stolen from you when you repeatedly do things that you really don't have to do. A couple of minutes here, a couple of minutes there, they all add up. Just like a dripping tap, many of us let our time dribble down the drain without a second thought. The five-minute phone call that turns into 15, the extra ten minutes in bed, the extra trip to school with forgotten homework. In the past you might have been forgiven for thinking that these little droplets of time were insignificant and of no value. Now you have been educated in the worth and scarcity of time, you know different.

In 1976 we were told in no uncertain terms the consequences of a neglected dripping tap. Did you know that it can waste between 30 and 200 litres of water a day? The same is true of your time: lost seconds and minutes add up to hours, days, weeks and months.

Tip! *Keep a mini sewing kit handy for those emergency repairs.*

The Amazing Disappearing Act

As your time drips into the sewers, it vanishes with the stealth and bemusing predictability of David Copperfield in a disappearing act. But unlike the illusionist, who'll be back to entertain us another day, your time has well and truly gone into a Wookey Hole from whence there is no return. Only a delusionist would think it's coming back anytime soon.

You're on a tight budget of 24 hours. You can't waste anything. Where is your time going? Where can you save time to make time for the things you want to do?

It's often said that time is money. If you went to the bank manager to get a loan, she'd want to know how you were going to pay it back. She'd want sight of an income-and-expenditure statement before she'd give you a penny. She'd need to know what your outgoings were. Unless she could see that you had the means to pay the bank back, she wouldn't give you anything. She'd send you off with your tail between your legs, telling you to come back when you'd got a grip on your budgeting. You need a handle on how you spend your time, just like you need a handle on how you spend your money.

From the Mouths of Mums:

'I really can't understand it, but the more time I have, the less I get done. When the children were at home I was busy all the time, I had to be really organized and even though I was exhausted I did seem to get a lot done. Now they are at school I don't seem to get anything done, it feels like my jobs expand to fit the time I've got.'

Here we see a perfect demonstration of Parkinson's Law in action. This law states that work will expand to fit the time we have available. It's definitely happening to this mum, who has no idea where her time is going. She certainly hasn't stopped to think about why she's in her dilemma. She seems to have lost her focus. She talks as if she has no control over her situation.

Because she doesn't know where her time is going she feels disempowered. Her time is seeping away. She has no real feel for how long tasks are taking her; things just fill her day. If she stood back and examined where her day was going in more detail she would probably find that, with focus, she could get a lot more done and feel a lot more in control.

In essence we have to think about where we focus our efforts. If you found yourself agreeing with a lot of the statements in the 'something to think about' list and they did indeed make you go, 'umm...' or 'oh dear!', you're probably not thinking enough about what you focus on. If you feel frazzled and dissatisfied with life, then chances are you're not focusing on anything that's particularly important to you either. Not really the ideal way to live your life. It's not uncommon, though. When we have children their lives take over ours. We're too busy sorting school uniforms, making packed lunches, cleaning, doing the laundry, shopping for food, helping with homework and perhaps holding down a job out of the house to think for even a moment about what we're actually doing. We just do it and meanwhile our time is disappearing rapidly.

Tip! Always put the cordless phone back on its base – or stick to a corded one.

The Key to Time Management

And here we have it, the Key to Time Management: the fundamental and overwhelming truth is that you can't manage time. I know you might be thinking 'I've paid good money for this book on managing my time, and now you're telling me that time can't be managed, thanks a bundle!' Before you rush out for a refund, let me explain where I'm going with this.

Whether you like it or not, time can't be tamed, trained or restrained. It keeps on ticking away regardless of what you choose to do with it. Please, though, remember what they say: 'The truth will set you free.'

Prepare to be set free as you learn the watch words of time management. Guess what? Neither of them is time or management. The need-to-know magic words are Choice and Focus. Just like the magic words of etiquette, please and thank you, begin using Choice and Focus as the basis for getting what you want and suddenly things will start appearing in your life, like loads more time.

If you look in the dictionary, time is defined as *'The continuous passage of existence in which events pass from a state of potentiality in the future, through the present, to a state of finality in the past.'*

Time is continuous. It stops, waits or slows down for no one. Like frizzy hair on a damp day, it can't be managed. What can be managed, though, is the series of events that we choose to focus on as we pass through time. The only thing in life that we really have any control over is what we choose to do in any given moment. All that time does is tell you when these activities take place.

For me, time is like the punctuation in this book. The full stops and commas prevent one sentence from running into the next. It separates ideas and thoughts by providing visual markers, letting you know when to take a pause or a breath before moving on. It helps you make sense of things. Well, at least I hope it does. Time is the same. It lets you know when things are happening and how long they are taking. It provides structure and a common marker for everyone. It assists us in making sense of our world, by providing us with a framework to organize ourselves around. We use it to let us know when to do particular activities. Pick the children up at 3.15, go to bed at 11.30, get up at

7.00. That's it, that's all time does. Like a ruler, protractor or the dreaded bathroom scales, it's a tool for measurement. Like them, sadly, it can't be managed.

Making the most of the time you've got is about making choices about what to focus on. This choice of focus will influence what happens to you in the present and in the future. To think of it another way, time is like an empty wardrobe. Your life is the clothes that you decide to hang in it.

You can change your clothes (or your focus), but you can't change the wardrobe.

Regardless of what events or clothes you choose to put on the rail of your life, the wardrobe never changes. Time ticks away at exactly the same pace, so getting some clarity about what you are choosing to focus on right now will dramatically and positively impact how much time you have. 'Fantastic,' you cry, 'but how will I do it?' The Eye of Time is the tool that will help you get this focus.

Tip! *Negotiate some working-from-home time to cut down on commuting.*

The Eye of Time

This is quite possibly the most fabulous tool for assisting you to pinpoint what you're choosing to focus on right now. Are you getting everything done that you want to? Does what you focus on every day reflect what is really important to you in your life? Interesting questions, let's investigate further.

The Eye of Time works in the same way as your own eyes. By taking visual data from all around us, it creates a full Technicolor visual representation of what we see at any given moment. By taking information and data about what we focus our attention on, it creates a picture of what our life looks like at any given moment in time. It provides us with a snapshot of what we are focusing on, what we are choosing to do.

Ever heard the phrase, 'You get what you focus on'? Just as you see what your eyes focus on, you get in your life what you choose to focus your attention on.

Your focus becomes your reality. The Eye of Time helps you get 20/20 clarity about how your life looks right now. If you're feeling out of control, then my guess is that what you're focusing on isn't the right stuff, and doesn't reflect what's important to you. The Eye of Time has four different spheres of vision and focus.

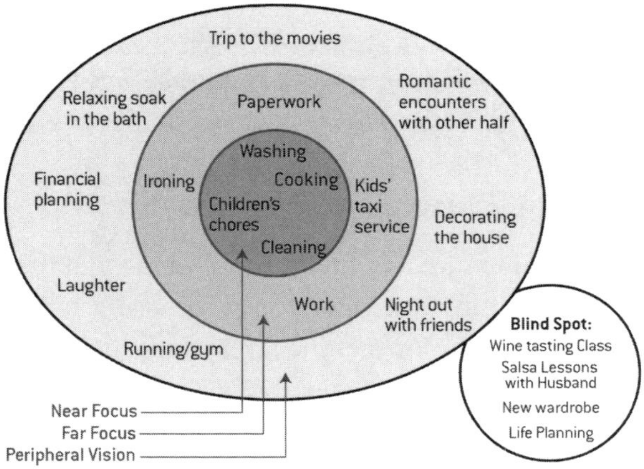

The Eye of Time for Manic Martha

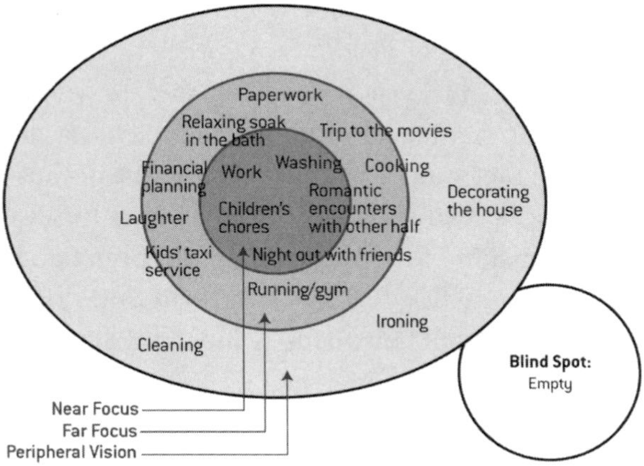

The Eye of Time for Perfect Paula

Near Focus

The first sphere of vision is near focus. We can't help but focus on activities in this sphere, because they are right in front of our face. We feel we have to deal with them immediately. People have different activities in their near focus: washing and ironing, feeding a small baby, working all hours, running children around in the car, cooking. The list is endless and everyone's is different. It's true to say, though, that our attention is taken by what we choose to focus on. If we don't make a conscious effort to focus our attention on something in particular, then random items will pop into our near-focus viewfinder.

If you take a peek at Manic Martha's near focus, you'll see that it's filled with drudge. She constantly complains that she doesn't have any time. It's because she's not making choices about what she's bringing into this sphere of vision. Sometimes as mums we get trapped in tunnel vision, focusing only on what we find in front of our face, not choosing to look at anything else. I've met mums who are distraught because their whole focus seems to be on dreary things like washing, ironing, making food, clearing up, shopping and reacting to crises. They feel stuck in a rut and don't know how to get out. Their focus is indeed their reality and they feel trapped by it.

From the Mouths of Mums:

'I do nothing but tend to, talk to or think about my children. I have no time for me. I can't remember the last time I had a grown-up conversation. When I talk to other adults all we talk about is our children. What size shoes they take now, or the latest piece of gossip from the school playground. I'm so used to focusing on the children, when my husband took me out for dinner I pointed out three "woof woofs" en route to the restaurant. When we got there habit practically forced me to stretch across the table and chop up his fillet steak into morsels. How sad have I become; surely there's more to life than this?'

'Be careful which rut you choose, you'll be stuck in it for a long time.' ROAD SIGN IN NEW YORK

It's all too easy to get stuck in a rut and focus on one aspect of life. If you do, life can become a dreary, dull place. Ralph Waldo Emerson once said that we become what we think about. For a number of years I feared I would morph into a dirty nappy or pile of washing. Why? That's all I seemed to have in my near focus. Perfect Paula seems able to focus on more exciting things. The trick is to be able to bring the things you want to get done into near focus. Then move all the things you don't want to be doing out of sight.

For example, Paula brings cleaning into her near focus for just 20 minutes every day. By keeping on top of things, her house is always tidy, leaving her free to focus on other activities. Manic Martha, on the other hand, has cleaning in her near focus all the time. This is because her lack of systematic planning and routine means her house is always a mess. Mess and cleaning are always part of her near focus.

People who don't manage their time well have *static focus*. They choose to focus only on what's in front of them. People like Paula have *dynamic focus*. They are able to change constantly what's in near focus, paying attention to tasks that they have consciously decided to undertake at that given moment in time.

Far Focus

This sphere contains all the stuff you can see, but it seems more distant than near focus. Quite often for mums, so many things are fighting to get into near focus there's just no capacity to see beyond it.

Sometimes mums forget to bring the items that sit in this sphere into near focus and they sit neglected.

For Martha it's paperwork, and we all know what happens when you don't focus on your paperwork for any length of time. You miss the letter telling you that you need to make a costume for the Christmas play. Your child ends up being the only one with nothing to wear on the big day. How bad do you feel? Perfect Paula, for her part, is able to take romance from her far focus and bring it into her near focus when she wants to look at it. Romantic encounters are only found in Manic Martha's peripheral vision. You've got to have some space in front of you to see out this far. You need to be able to look up to see the horizon. Not always easy with a ball and chain round your left leg and a two-year-old hanging from the other. When you're down on the floor of life, up close and personal with small human beings, it can be difficult to look out into the other spheres of your vision.

Peripheral Vision

In your peripheral vision are the things you're aware of but not seeing very clearly. For Manic Martha, it's that night out with the girls that hasn't happened for months and is looking unlikely to materialize. As is the trip to the movies with her husband. He hasn't seen her wearing lipstick or anything other than baggy leggings for at least a year. Is it any wonder romantic encounters are slipping into her blind spot? In Paula's peripheral vision we see ironing. She's given it to someone else to do, so no longer has to look at it, how fabulous.

Paula is very careful with her money, so can afford to pay for an ironer. Martha, on the other hand, can't. She does things like leave her car parked in a space for too long, and gets a £30 ticket. She then forgets to pay the fine and incurs a penalty for another £30. By doing things at the last minute she usually ends up paying considerably more for everything. Her approach to life costs her more in all sorts of ways, not just in lost time.

Blind Spots

This is all the stuff you just can't see any more. You might even have to think hard to remember what it looks like. I spoke to a mum once who said that having fun was in her blind spot. It had been there for so long she couldn't even think of what a fun activity might be for her. Things we've put off can often revert to our blind spot. It's all those things we've not been paying attention to. Like a car that comes from nowhere into your near-side mirror just as you're about to pull out, things that lurk in your blind spot have a nasty habit of jumping out on you when you least expect them. Having an awareness of what's in your blind spot, and positioning your mirrors accordingly, are crucial in the navigation of your life.

Tip! *Invest in a timer or stop watch, then set time-limits for a particular job and stick to it.*

What Are You Choosing to Focus On?

If you were to think generally about how you spend your time, where would the majority of it be? What would you be focusing on? Just take a moment to think about your focus on a typical day and plot it onto the Eye of Time.

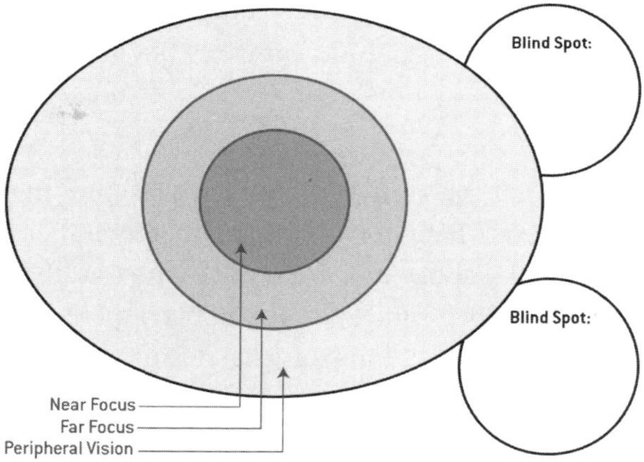

My Eye of Time

Any shocks? Any surprises? Are there some things that aren't in your focus that you'd like to be? Are there some things in your focus that you'd rather were somewhere else? Are you focusing on what's really important to you?

What tends to happen is that if we don't take control of what we focus on we just look at whatever jumps up in front of our face. Think about the following questions in relation to your world:

What am I focusing on?
What's in my near focus?
What's in my far focus?
What's in my peripheral vision?
Where are my blind spots, what am I not focusing on at all?

Some mums who've answered these questions for me have come to the following conclusions:

- They have in fact been spending the vast majority of their days going round and round in circles, like a dog chasing its tail, achieving not very much of any significance.
- Most of the things that they once held dear – their dreams and aspirations – have become firmly lodged in their blind spot.
- Most of what falls into their near focus is a pile of dull and mundane chores. The highlight of the day is falling into bed feeling dizzy, exhausted and confused.

Well that's no good, is it? We want fabulous days. We want meaningful days. We want quality time. In the next chapter, we'll be using a bold and daring palette to paint a picture of the kind of day you want to be having. Before we do, let's just finish getting to the bottom of where all your time is going right now.

Does What You Focus on Reflect What Is of Value to You?

How good do you feel about your life right now? How much control do you feel you have? The reason many mums get frustrated with their lot is that, although their families are very important to them, they become bogged down in the mechanics of running a home. This becomes their only focus. This is true for working mums and stay-at-home mums alike. There never seems to be enough time to get all the things done that would allow you to feel like you are leading a well-rounded life. Just like our eyes need 20/20 vision to be able to focus properly, we need the equivalent of 20/20 vision in our life focus if we want to enjoy it to the full. If you feel like your life is a blur and lacks focus and clarity, perhaps it's time you had your eyes tested. So I'm going to ask you to take the Eye of Time test to work out how focused your life is right now on what really matters to you. Are you feeling 20/20 or a little bit blurry?

Tip! Send texts and e-mails to large groups to save time on phone calls – particularly if you're prone to chatting

The Eye of Time Life Focus and Values Focus

Take a look at the two eyes on the next page and on page 56.

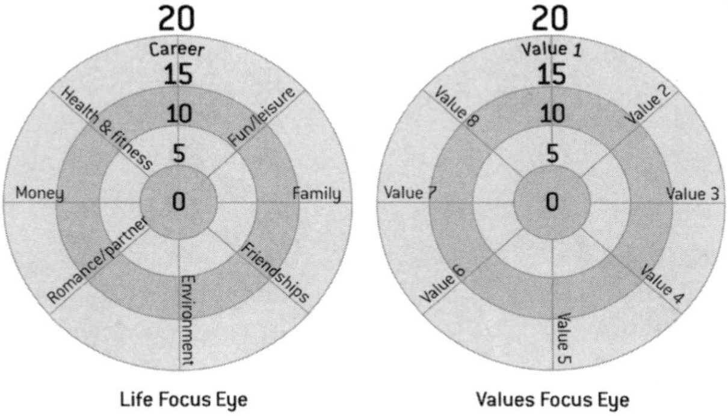

Eye of Time Life Focus and Values Focus

Life Focus Eye

The left eye in the illustration represents your life focus. This eye is split into eight segments that represent eight areas of your life: career, fun and leisure, family, friendships, environment, romance/partner, money, and health and fitness. If you think of something that is more important than these, or if you want to add another segment, feel free. It's your life.

When you are happy with the segments, give yourself a score out of 20 for each. A score of 20 means that you are completely happy with this aspect of your life focus. A score of 0 would mean that you are totally unhappy with this aspect of your life focus. Plot the scores onto the Life Focus Eye. The centre of the eye represents a score of 0 and the outer circle of the eye represents a score of 20. Notice how close the segments are to 20. Join up the plot lines. Then shade the area outside the plot line in black (see example below). The black area represents what you're not able to see in your life right now.

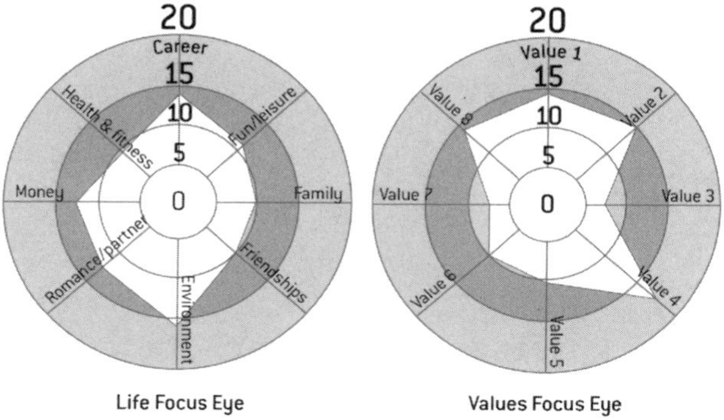

What can't I see in my life right now?

Values Focus Eye

The right eye represents your values, the things that are most important to you in your life. Most of us live our lives never really having thought about what is truly important to us. If one of your values is fun, yet you spend all your days focusing on dull mundane tasks, you'll be feeling dissatisfied with life. Our values come from inside us and influence our behaviour and actions. As sure as a woman on a diet wants chocolate, your values need to be satisfied and focused on.

Do you know what your values are? If not, you need to work them out, and write them down. There are no right or wrong values. They will be personal to you. To give you some ideas, here are some examples of values people have told me about in the past:

Integrity, fun, personal development, honesty, assertiveness, courage, creativity, friendliness, spirituality, energy, independence, loyalty, determination, hard work, generosity, happiness, playfulness, perfection, reliability, punctuality, optimism.

Tip! *Buy a sound-activated device for your keys – think how much time you've wasted over the years looking for them.*

To help you decide what your values are, here are some questions to think about:

- What issues do you get on your soapbox about? What values do they reflect?
- What makes you cross? What value is being violated to make you feel this way?
- If you asked your friends and family to describe you, what words would they use? How do these descriptions reflect your values?
- What is something that you would never do, lines you would never cross? Which values would you be violating by crossing these lines?
- In the past, when faced with tough decisions, what actions have you taken? What values did these actions reflect?

When you have your list, decide what your eight most important values are. Write them on the segments of the eye. Score each one out of 20 and join them up in the same way as you did with the Life Focus Eye.

Look at both eyes. How close are you to 20/20 vision? Are you finding time to look at what's important to you, or are you treading water? If it's the latter, let's find you some more time to look at what you really want to focus on.

How Do You Get More Time to Focus on Other Things?

If we were to start with some really basic investigations about where all your time is going, would you have any idea whatsoever how long you spend on normal daily activities? Have you the slightest clue about where the leaks, drips and cracked pipes are in your system? If you were to hazard a guess at how long you spend per day, or per week, on some of the activities below, would you really know? Based on conversations I've had with many people, my guess is that your answers wouldn't be too accurate.

What kind of a handle do you have on your time? Is it leaking away because you're not paying attention to it?

- How much time a day do you spend on the telephone?
- How much time do you spend watching television?
- How long do you spend in the shower?
- How long do you spend at (paid) work?
- How long do you engage in idle chit-chat?
- How long do you spend exercising?

- How long do you spend preparing food?
- How long do you spend shopping?
- How much time do you spend playing with your children?
- How much time do you spend talking to your partner?

If you struggle to answer, or know deep down that your answers are at best a guess, you're not alone.

Most people have no idea. Alternatively, some people think they know, but when they assess accurately how much time they're spending it turns out to be a lot longer or shorter than they originally thought. When I ask people how long they stand in the shower each day, they invariably say just a couple of minutes. When they subsequently make a conscious note of how long the shower lasts, it's always much more. Odd as it may seem, unless you know the answers to these questions, it's hard to define what you might want to do in the future. Lots of people tell me that they want to spend more time with their children. So I ask them the question, 'How much time do you spend with your children now?' They rarely know. Most people are surprised to see where their time goes when they examine what they spend it on.

From the Mouths of Mums:

'With two small children and a four-days-a-week job, I always thought that I had no time, but when I made a realistic assessment of how I

spent my days I found that I was watching TV for at least 8 hours a week. I would just sit and watch it in the evening when the kids had finally gone to bed. I didn't really think about how long I was spending on this, and that over the course of a week it really adds up. I'm not saying I don't want to watch TV any more, because I love my telly and I find it a great way of relaxing, but it has made me aware of how much time I have got, and that I could perhaps do something else with it, because there are a lot of things in my house that aren't getting done right now.'

The Top-20 Drips from the Tap of Time

When it comes to leaking time, there's a lot more dripping away than we think. Just to get you thinking where your drips might be, here are some of the key culprits. This is a veritable hall of fame, a rogues' gallery of villains, because like it or not these stinkers are stealing your time. They do it with the stealth and transparency of the Invisible Man. You probably hadn't even realized what was being taken from right under your nose. Drip, drip, drip:

1. Watching TV
2. Unnecessary phone calls and talking on the phone for too long
3. Drop-in guests
4. Waiting in queues with nothing to do
5. Reading newspapers and magazines

6. Constantly checking email/reading junk mail
7. Looking for things you've misplaced (papers, car keys, etc.)
8. Unnecessary chit-chat and gossip in the playground and other places
9. Worrying about things you cannot control
10. Time stuck in traffic
11. Returning home for things you've forgotten
12. Clearing up after others
13. Coffee, tea and cigarette breaks
14. Thinking about doing things rather than just doing them
15. Compulsively sorting mail and paying bills
16. Surfing the net
17. Childcare with no breaks
18. Endless trips to the shops for things you've forgotten
19. Saying yes to tasks you should have said no to
20. Being a perfectionist

Just think, if you could save five minutes a day on just 12 of these activities, you'd have an extra hour. Now what could you do with that?

What Would You Do with a 25th Hour?

I'm not trying to make you salivate here, but imagine you did have more time. You've seen how easy it might be to create an extra hour. Just by noticing where your time is seeping away and doing those things less, you get to reclaim time. It doesn't have to be hard, either. Spending five minutes less on the phone, would it kill you? Dropping one coffee break a day is positively not going to harm you. So, just to motivate you, here's an incentive: I'm going to give you an extra hour, the Magic Hour. I'm going to ask you to imagine for a moment that every day has 25 hours, not a measly 24. Yes, imagine that it is indeed your lucky day. The Time Fairy has paid you a visit, and left you a Magic Hour under your pillow. What would you do with it? How would you use it? This is a question I often ask people.

The interesting thing I notice when I ask mums about their Magic Hour is that they usually reply with something fairly simple, like, 'I'd really love to have five minutes to myself.' If you had one hour every day, you could do that 12 times over. Imagine doing something that you really wanted to do 12 times, in just one day. Marvellous. Never have I heard anybody say that they want to climb Mount Everest, bungee jump from the Empire State Building or sing at Sydney Opera House. Wonderful as those things are, such is the life of a frazzled mother it's more likely they'd choose to take a Pilates class, go for a bike ride or sit down and have quality time with the children in their newly acquired extra hour. The activities people come up with for their Magic Hour are, on the whole, quite achievable. Activities that, with a bit of focus, we could fit in. Start thinking about what you'd do with your Magic Hour. You're about to create it.

Getting to Grips with Your Drips

It's not uncommon to prepare an expenditure statement for your money so you can manage your finances and spending.

Why not do the same for your time? Last week you worked out a value for your time. Would you really just fritter it away if it was worth something? Wouldn't you want to know where it was going? Your mission for this week, should you choose to accept it, is to get to grips with your drips.

Work out where your time goes. We are going to detect and plug your leaks. (How right was I when I said time was like your pelvic floor?) This will do for you what the panache of a plumber would do for your broken pipe work. For those of you whose mains have burst, the Water Board is on its way.

> Tip! *Keep a well-stocked medical kit with essential supplies, thermometer, etc. so you're not rushing round in the middle of the night trying to find a 24-hour chemist.*

Doing the Diagnostics – What Time Traps Are You Falling Into?

Exercise Days One to Five

On page 66 there's a log sheet. This is going to be your blueprint for success. Here you will keep a note of exactly how you spend your time each day. Every 30 minutes, stop for a moment and note down what you've been doing for the past half hour. Do it all day for the next five days. I often do this with my clients who feel they are out of control and need more time. Unsurprisingly their first response to this exercise is, 'I don't have time to do this!' 'Here I am,' they say, 'asking you to make my life less cumbersome. Here you are, giving me another thing to do, that I don't have time for. Aghhhhhhh!!' My response is always clear and resounding: 'You don't have time not to do this.'

If you don't respect the Second Truth of Time Management – 'the only way to get more time is to know how you spend what you've got' – you're not going to get as much time as you possibly could. It's a critical step on the path to getting more time. Don't do it and you'll carry on encountering the same problems. Do it and you'll be on the way to a better life. It's simple and it's a choice you can make.

Einstein once said that the definition of madness was to keep on doing the same things again and again, expecting different results. I think what the great man meant was: do something different. Come on, ladies, listen up, get a grip and work out what you're doing now so you can start doing something different. Start getting different, and better, results in your life.

To get yourself started, make a few copies of the log sheet. Alternatively, make up a rough one of your own on a piece of paper. Keep it with you at all times so it's easy for you to fill it in. We don't want to have to waste time looking for it now, do we?! For the next five days, every 30 minutes fill in what you are doing.

Also note down how you are feeling. It's quite an eye-opener to pay attention to what activities make you feel good and what activities don't make you feel so good. If certain things make you feel happy or excited, you might decide to start doing them more. Conversely, things that make you feel like you've been dragged through a hedge backwards could be culled. If you're interrupted during a task, note the nature of the interruption. You know the kind of thing I mean, the cry of, 'Mummy, will you wipe my bottom?', 'I need a drink', or the doorbell chimes. Note in the last column how long each activity takes. For all you ExecuMums, why not do a similar exercise just for your work day? The results could astound you.

Exercise Days Six and Seven

When you have completed the chart you will have a much better view of where your time is going. Having it all written down allows you to look at things from a different perspective. It's a bit like being in a helicopter looking down on your life, rather than being stuck in the day-to-day fray. To get that bird's-eye view, over the next two days do a tally of where you spend your time by filling in the table on page 67. Calculate how much time you spent on each thing you did over the five days. Add any categories that I've missed. This isn't definitive, it's just a guide. Look through your list and ask yourself, where is my time leaking away? Also notice how different activities made you feel. Which ones are losing you time? Which ones are sapping your emotional energy?

Drip Diagnostics for:

Day:

Time activity started	Activity	How are you feeling? What is your mental, emotional, physical state? E.g. tired, stressed, distracted, relevant observations	Interruptions	Duration in minutes

Activity	Total time spent	How much time does this lose me?	How does this activity make me feel?
Sleeping	35hrs.		relaxed
Eating	10-11		relaxed
Preparing and clearing up food	2 hrs		bored hated it
Shopping	4-5		bored. hate it
Working	7		bored hate it
Travelling to work	75		" "
Children's homework	—		—
Driving	1½		Enjoy
Children's school activities	—		—
Playing with the children	—		—
Dressing, bathing, putting to bed/general childcare	—		—
Personal care	3		relaxed
Watching TV	40.		relaxed
Relaxation and leisure	—		—
Exercise	—		—
Reading	2-3 hrs.		Exciting
Cleaning	1 hr.		boring
Running errands	—		
Washing and ironing	5 mins		boring
Internet	—		
Time with friends	—		
Time with partner	—		
Social phone calls	40 — 50 mins.		boring
Texting	1 hour		boring
E-mailing	—		

From the Mouths of Mums:

'When I filled out my log it made me realize that a lot of the time I was bringing work home, constantly checking emails and making odd phone calls. What I hadn't appreciated was just how much time this was taking up. I was doing this in what should really be my own time. It made me feel anxious and guilty because I wasn't spending quality time with my husband and children.'

'I've always been a bit of a gas bag, but it really brought it home to me how much I talk when I discovered that I never spend less than 20 minutes on the phone, and I make a lot of phone calls, more than I realized. Talking on the phone makes me happy. Being late for other things because I've spent too long on the phone makes me feel stressed.'

As you analyse your five days, really think hard about where your time has been going. Where are the holes, cracks and crevices that your time drops down, never to be seen again? Identify your top 10 leaks, then name and shame them in your very own rogues' gallery.

My Top Ten Leaks

1. TV
2. Eating
3. Sleep.
4. Avoidance / putting things off.
5. lacking structure. / No timetable.
6. No focus.
7. No structure for day or for kids
8. lazyness + tiredness
9.
10.

As you write them down, and hang your head in shame, ask yourself the million-dollar question, 'Where am I spending time that is costing me dear, because it's denying me the opportunity to do something else?' When you've got the answer, ask yourself, 'How can I repair my leaks?' What are the things you could do differently next week to plug your leaks and gain more time?

Just think about it. If you could find six things that save ten minutes each, you'd have saved 60 minutes. You'd have that whole extra hour you were thinking about. What was it you said you wanted to do with it?

Six Actions to Plug My Leaks and Create a Magic Hour

So put your thinking cap on and get your creative juices flowing. Don't save them just for the kids' craft projects. If you're stuck, take inspiration from the tips in this book. Try some of them. See how much time you can claw back.

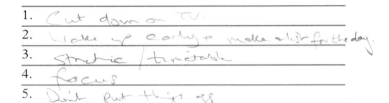

1. Cut down on TV.
2. Wake up early & make a list for the day.
3. Structure / timetable
4. Focus
5. Don't put things off
6. Have set eating times..

Tip! *Never be kept on hold. Agree a time to ring back or leave your phone number and a message.*

As you plug your leaks, what you're doing is choosing to change what you focus on. You're making better choices about what you bring into your near focus. If you want to have more time, you have to make better choices. To make better choices, you need to know what your options are. Before your very eyes, you've seen how easy it is to pick up an extra hour. All it takes is noticing what you've been doing, and then choosing to do something different.

Is one extra hour enough? Do you want more? What if you really could live the life of your dreams and have it all? A life where you are doing what is really important to you, how would that be? Well, you can. Don't settle for just one extra hour, ask for more. Get the life you want. If you want to know how, read on, because this is just the tip of the iceberg.

Tip! *Put the children's school uniforms out the night before. Even better, get them to do it. .*

Actions for Week Two

- Complete your Eye of Time (ten minutes).
- Complete your Life Focus Eye and Values Focus Eye (20 minutes).
- Fill out your Drip Diagnostics time log (ongoing days one to five).
- Identify your top-ten time leaks (ten minutes).
- Identify six things you can do to plug your time leaks (ten minutes).
- Do the six things (this will save you time).
- Give yourself the gift of an extra hour. Choose something to do in your hour. Commit to doing it and put everything in place to make sure that it happens (ten minutes' preparation plus your hour).

Tip! *Record programmes to watch later, cutting out the adverts.*

Summary

- To save time you must first know how you spend it.
- Like the backs of your earrings, lose time and you'll never find it again.

- The key to time management is choice and focus.
- If you want to get more done, stop and consider what you focus on during your day. If what you are doing isn't productive, choose to focus on something else.
- Does what you focus on reflect what's important to you?
- If not, work out your values and choose to focus on activities that reflect them.
- Write down everything you do for a week, then gaze in wonderment at how much time you've wasted doing things that aren't important to you.
- Choose to eradicate the things that are wasting your time and replace them with things you'd rather be doing.
- Give yourself a fabulous reward for finding extra time in your life.

Tip! *Tumble-dry clothes on the low heat setting until the washing is just dry. Get the washing out while it's still warm and at its most co-operative. Place each item on a flat surface and smooth out with your hands before carefully folding it to be put away.*

Week Three

How Much Time Do You Want?

An Ode to What You'd Do with More Time

If there were no limit to the hours in each day,
What a treat it would be to while them away.
I'd clip all my toenails,
And sort out my socks,
Whilst quietly sipping a gin on the rocks.
I'd remove all the rubbish from under the stairs,
Then go and shave off all my under-arm hairs.
Clear out my in-tray,
And sort out the mail,
Eat up my lunch at the pace of a snail.
See to my roots, buy some new boots,
Shop for a dress, and several new suits.
Have my hair styled,
Get my fingernails filed,
Go buy that cream that I need for my piles.
I know it sounds daft,
With the kids I'd do craft,
And I'd fix that door where there's always a draught.
If it's all the same,
We might play a game,
I'd love to get one out the Cellophane,
But for once I'd be spending quality time,
And guess what, it doesn't cost me a dime.
I might even find that there's no need to shout,
As I slowly and carefully sort my kids out.

Time Truths 1 2 3 4 5 6 7

Know what you want, then you'll find time to look for it

How Much Time Do You Want?

Whoopee, you've fixed your leaky plumbing, you've learned how to create an extra hour, and you've tasted what it's like to be more in control of your life. Yum, it's as good as a carton of Ben & Jerry's Cookie Dough ice-cream. It just shows, doesn't it, what's possible with relative ease if you take a look at where your time is going. When you know what time traps you're falling into, you can pick yourself up, dust yourself down and claim it all back.

What would you say, though, if you knew there were ways to get even more time, even more of what you want out of life? I bet you'd want to know what that was, right this second. Well, get your head around Time Truth Number Three and that's exactly what will happen. So let's move on and start thinking about how much time you really want, and find not just an extra hour, but time to create the kind of days that, right now, you can only dream about.

Shop till You Drop

Imagine for a moment that you've been given carte blanche to go on a shopping trip. On this trip you're buying time and you can fill your basket with as much of it as you want. Yes, this is the point where you get to dream, and you get to be demanding. We're not talking about just an extra hour. We're talking about the amount of time that you really deserve and desire. You'll be filling your shopping basket to the brim with whatever you want. By deciding what you want in your life, rather than just accepting what it throws at you, you'll be able to transform the Eye of Time you created last week into your ideal Eye of Time this week.

The new Eye of Time will represent the day, nay life, you want to be leading. It will better reflect all those things that you've identified as being important to your life focus and your value focus. Instead of your day being a set of events that just seems to happen randomly to you, you are going to start making some informed choices about what you want in your focus.

From the Mouths of Mums:

'I'm so busy I don't have time to think about what I want.'

The Shopping List of Life

Deciding how much time you want is more like shopping than you might imagine. How many times have you been shopping without a list? After pushing and shoving your trolley around the supermarket you end up returning home laden with a whole bagful of goods you didn't want. As you unpack and put them away, you realize there's nothing for supper and you're missing the essential item you went out for, toilet rolls.

Armed with a list you are so much more likely to purchase what you set out to buy. Why? As you cruise the supermarket aisles you know exactly what you are looking for.

If you think of life like a shopping trip, most people's baskets are filled with all sorts of things they don't want or need. Why? They haven't made a list to focus on what they do want. Most of the people I talk to feel like they are living in a reactive state. They frequently tell me that they feel like fire-fighters, always dealing with emergencies. They certainly don't believe they have any control. The messy picture that manifests itself as their life comes about because they haven't thought through what they really want to focus on. They've been so busy focusing on what life throws at them, they've never been able to think about what they would prefer to look at.

Tip! *Do small jobs as they come up; don't put them off.*

Choose What's Going on Your Shopping List

If the focus making up your reality isn't what you truly want, then it's time to start making some new choices about what you're focusing on. If you don't, then your focus, just like a shopping basket without a list, will fill up with whatever gets tossed into it. Choose to live like this and your reality will be chaos and fire-fighting. Make a choice to become the architect of your own activity by creating a shopping list for your life, and you'll be able to create the days of your dreams.

From the Mouths of Mums:

'I'm amazed at how much difference it makes just sitting down and getting clear about what I

want to be doing with my time. It makes me feel more centred, and like there's a slim chance I'll get done what I want, not just what everyone else wants. Before I did this I felt like a slave and really disempowered, just jumping to everyone else's demands and never focusing any time on me and what I wanted. Quite honestly, on reflection, I now realize that I spent most of my time moaning about how disorganized my life was, without ever stopping to think about how I really wanted it to be instead.'

Truth Three categorically states: 'Know what you want from your time, then you'll find time to look for it.' As this mum explains, knowing what you want is key to actually getting it. So what do you want in your basket?

Fill Your Basket with What You Want

Let me share an example from my own life. Something that I had written on my personal shopping list, and that was in my near focus before my first daughter was born, was writing a book. This book would reveal the chilling truth about pregnancy and childbirth. I took action towards making this happen. I bought a writing course, thinking I would have free time to study and write in between baby feeds. A foolish notion if ever I heard one.

Needless to say, when Hannah arrived, other things dropped into my near focus. Like a wet bar of soap in the bath, the idea of a book slipped further and further away from me, until finally it dissolved. It only came into my peripheral vision for occasional glimpses, before slipping back out again, having barely been given a once-over.

Like many of the dreams and aspirations I had before babies, my book dropped off the radar screen. My antennae picked up stronger signals from other areas of my life, and these became my focus. Feeding Callum, ironing a shirt, spending three hours getting nits out of Laura's hair, that was the stuff my life was made of. That was my focus. Every now and again I would make a glib comment that one day, when I had more time, I was going to write a book about pregnancy. As time ticked on I well and truly forgot that I'd ever even contemplated the idea. My prenatal aspiration was relegated to my blind spot, as is the fate of so many of our dreams and poorly performing football teams.

I'm glad to say that, ten years on, I have managed to produce the epic work you read now. Let me assure you, with three children, a husband who works long hours and a house to run, it didn't happen all by itself. So how was it that I eventually got round to finding time to write a book? It began with a clear view of what I wanted to create, coupled with a desire to spend time on it. I had to move some of the dross taking up my near focus out of the limelight. It had to go into my peripheral vision, so I could make space for something else: writing my book and creating my coaching company.

As a person with a natural predisposition to disorganization, lack of structure and chaos, with little respect for time, believe me I had to learn how to do this. It did not come naturally. By nature I am a Manic

Martha, full of ideas but not much discipline to execute them. Now I know the Truths of Time Management and apply them rigorously to my own life, I know it's pretty much possible to achieve anything you want with your time. Even when weighed down by motherhood. My journey to time-management mastery all started with knowing what I wanted to focus on.

Five years before I wrote the book you're reading now, I took a good look at what I wanted in my focus. I wanted to run a business that would allow me to have real quality time with my family. In my near focus I didn't want housework. I wanted fun activities and quality time for me. I wanted a fulfilling career that allowed me to have a great work/life balance.

At that point I had no clue whatsoever how I would get this vision to be my reality. Let's face it, I was a full-time mum with three small children under the age of five. Most of my focus time was spent in bedlam. I was cooking, cleaning and tidying up, basically reacting to my children's needs. But I knew for sure that I wanted something more. Getting real clarity about what you want to focus on is the first step in allowing you to get back in the driving seat of your life.

> *Tip!* *Test children on times-tables or spellings on the way to school.*

With Your Basket Packed, Move to Planet Productivity

How can you get this type of clarity? You've spent a week ascertaining where all your time has been going to date. The big question to ask yourself now is, 'What do I want on my life shopping list?' If you want what's in your near focus to look different, what changes will you need to make in order to start seeing your day pan out in a more productive way? As you ponder this, you are taking a monumental leap from the world of reaction into the word of proactivity. On Planet Proactive, local residents are in control of their lives. They call the shots. Believe me when I say this is the place you want to be living. So fasten your seatbelt and prepare for blast-off, as you create a new picture of how you want to spend your time.

Tip! Mark children's socks with their initials (ah, the joys of permanent marker!) or different coloured threads so they get kept together and put back into the right child's wardrobe.

See the World through Your New Eye of Time

Let's turn your Eye of Time on its head. Let's transform it into one that reflects what you want your life to look like. Fill the Eye of Time in again. This time, though, not in reactive mode, but in proactive mode. Instead of asking questions about how you currently spend time, ask yourself a set of new, empowering questions about how you want to spend your time.

Draw out a new Eye of Time, a new Life Focus Eye and a new Values Focus Eye. As you do so, think about the changes you would like to see in what you are focusing on right now.

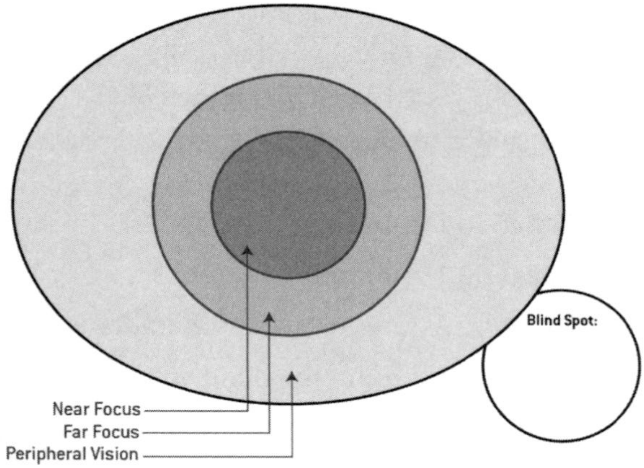

My desired Eye of Time

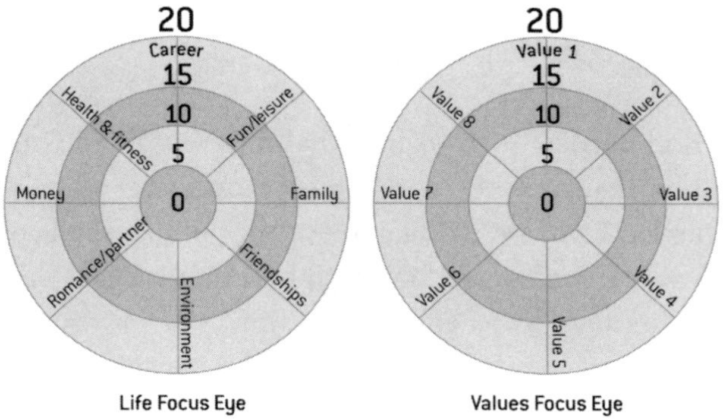

Eye of Time Life Focus and Values Focus

Where would you prefer your focus to be? Think about this particularly in relation to the things that are important to you. If you had the equivalent of 20/20 vision in your Life Focus and your Values Focus, doing only things that reflect what is really important to you, what would your Eye of Time look like?

Consider the questions below:

- What do I want in my near focus?
- What do I want in my far focus?
- What do I want in my peripheral vision?
- What do I want in my blind spot?
- What activities need to be on my Eye of Time, so my personal values come into focus?
- If I were spending time on things that were of value to me, what score would I want to achieve out of 20 in each segment of my Life Focus Eye and my Values Focus Eye?

If your ideal seems somewhat different from your current reality, don't worry. Just begin to get some clarity around what you'd like to see happening in all areas of your focus: near, far, peripheral and blind spots. If your days were going well, think about what things would be in focus for you. Would the ironing be in your blind spot and a visit to the gym be in your focus? Would a little real quality time doing craft with the children be in your focus, and time thinking about work be in your peripheral vision? It's your life, so you decide what you want it to look like.

Tip! *Make packed lunches the night before – or, even better, get the children to do their own.*

From Manic to Marvellous

Now you've got your ideal Eye of Time, you can start finding ways to make it your reality. Knowing what you want is at the heart of Truth Number Three. This is something that I have found to be true again and again.

People who know what they want stand a much higher chance of getting it than those who don't. Knowing what you want begins with vision, and when you possess the power of vision you have the touch-paper to relight the fire of your life and manifest what you want.

My own research into the lives of very successful 'MumPreneurs' (female entrepreneurs with children) has taught me that one of the key things they have in common is vision about what they want to achieve. The first step towards turning their business vision to reality is to make their goals, aspirations and dreams really vivid in their mind's eye. This is an approach echoed by many other successful figures. It was Walt Disney who said, 'If you can dream it you can do it' and Eleanor Roosevelt who stated that the future would belong to those who believed in the power of their dreams. Bill Gates envisioned the crazy notion of putting a computer on every desk. This was at a time when most computers took up a room the size of China! If he could do it surely we can get ourselves through a day without losing the will to live? Well of course we can, and you've just taken the first step by writing down what you'd like your focus to be.

Are We There Yet?

Now, there might be the odd cynic among you who thinks this is a load of psychobabble. You may even question the value of spending precious time on this. Let me assure you, you have not got time not to think about this. If you're too busy to be bothered with dreaming, read on to find out how clarifying what you want can help you in your quest to get your time-management mayhem sorted.

"Would you tell me please, which way I ought to go from here?"

"That depends a good deal on where you want to get to," said the Cat.

"I don't much care where" – said Alice.

"Then it doesn't matter much which way you go," said the Cat.

ALICE'S ADVENTURES IN WONDERLAND – LEWIS CARROLL

Taking something from vision to reality is a little bit like going on a journey. There's some distance between where you are now and where you want to be. If you want to stand any chance of arriving at your destination, you need to know precisely where you are heading. For argument's sake, let's say you are going on a journey to a town called 'More Time'. Knowing that you want to get to 'More Time' isn't enough. You need details, an exact address, the house number, the street name and the postcode.

We all know what happens when you don't have the exact address, don't we? You end up driving round and round in circles getting very frustrated with your other half, while, like the Donkey from *Shrek,* your kids annoyingly squeak from the back, 'Are we there yet?'

Imagine what would happen if you got into a cab, the driver asked you where you wanted to go and your answer was, 'I'm not sure.' The poor guy (or gal) would have no idea where to take you. The same is true of our lives. If we don't tell ourselves exactly where we want to be, how can we ever expect to get there? That's why so many of us spend our time travelling round and round in a car called stress, on a constant diversion through a town called 'No Time'. We just don't know exactly, precisely, definitively where we want to be.

We haven't created a clear vision or defined what we want our Eye of Time to be focusing on and driving towards. Is it any wonder we never get anywhere?

Define Your Destination and Start Driving

So what do you need to do to get to destination 'More Time'? Simple, you decide exactly where in 'More Time' you want to go. Your new Eye of Time will give you some clarity about your destination. All you have to do now is get your map out and look for ways to get there. Plan your journey. Look for signs and landmarks along the way that point you in the right direction. Seek out things that move you towards your desired focus.

In my case, if I'm unsure about where I'm going, I use one of the most fabulous gadgets I've ever possessed. It's called a GPS Satellite Navigation System.

Without fail, it always gets me where I want to go. To get anywhere in the world the only thing I need to know when I switch it on is where I want it to take me. If I want to get to Johannesburg, I tell my Sat Nav and it finds the quickest route for me. Imagine if you just told it all the places that you didn't want to go: 'I don't want to go to Sydney, I don't want to go to New York, I don't want to go to Paris.' How on earth would it know to take you to Johannesburg? Knowing all the places you don't want to go is as helpful as serving tea from a chocolate tea pot. By defining your new Eye of Time you'll be able to drive out of the rut that is your frantic life, with the power of four-wheel drive.

You'll know where you're going.

Tip! *Put a little cleaning kit in the glove box of your car, and a plastic bag to collect rubbish.*

The Sat Nav of Your Brain

In our brains we have our very own satellite navigation system. It's called our RAS, the Reticular Activating System. It works in a similar way to a Sat Nav and helps us to bring into our focus the things we want. But, like a Sat Nav, the one thing it needs is a destination.

Where do you want your RAS to take you? It gets its information from our dreams, our vision, or a clear articulation of our desired focus. In short, what we tell it we want to spend our time on. You've just started the process by identifying what's on your ideal Eye of

Time. Once your RAS knows this, it begins to work in exactly the same way as a Sat Nav.

So how does this work? The RAS uses filters to seek out signs that give it a route to get to where you have told it you want to go. Formulate a clear destination for your life, and it will be sent at light-speed down the neural information superhighway to the computer that is your brain. Like a best friend, your grey matter is looking out for you. Your brain really wants to get you what you desire. Like an obedient dog who loves you unconditionally, it will roll over and obey. It just can't help itself, because that was what it was designed to do. (If only children, husbands and bosses were so co-operative!)

Train Your Brain to Take You in the Right Direction

Let me give you some examples of how this fabulous piece of headgear can be used. A little bit trite, I know, but something I'm sure all us ladies can identify with: finding the perfect shoes to go with an outfit. A couple of years ago I was invited to a wedding, for which of course I had to have a new outfit and shoes. Well, that's what I told my husband anyway!

I found myself a beautiful bright red dress and decided the perfect accompaniment would be a pair of beautiful bright red shoes. Now, I don't know if you've ever tried to buy a pair of red shoes. I certainly hadn't, and I thought they might be hard to find. How wrong I was, because my RAS came to my assistance. I seemed to notice red shoes everywhere. I saw them in shop windows, on other people's feet. Even Dorothy's ruby red slippers on the front cover of my daughter's copy of *The Wizard of Oz* caught my attention. My RAS was bringing what I wanted into my focus, because it knew what I was looking for.

Here's another one for you. Ever had that bizarre experience when you were a teenager in love, perhaps with a crush on Simon Le Bon or just the boy next door? Every song on the radio seemed to be about falling in love. Then the inevitable happened, your first love left you, and you were firmly in their blind spot. Did you notice something different, that every song on the radio was about being dumped, breaking up or separating? Now is it true that the DJs of the day were totally in tune with you and your emotional state, producing you a personal play list? Sorry to disappoint, but no, they weren't. This phenomenon was just your RAS at work, filtering for things that seemed to be of importance to you, and then getting you to pay attention to them.

You find yourself in a particular place – in love, lost, having a baby. In that moment these things are highly relevant to you, and your RAS automatically filters for information about them. Often without you realizing it's happening. This fabulous tool, harnessed correctly, can really assist you in focusing on and getting what you want. In our case, loads more time, please.

Tip! *Use the speed-dialling facility on your phone.*

A Health-and-safety Warning

A word to the wise: this headgear does come with a note of caution. In the hands of someone who doesn't know their RAS from their elbow, it's a dangerous piece of kit. 'How could that possibly be?' I hear you cry. How could something that sounds so fabulous possibly have a fault? The major pitfall of our RAS is that it can be easily misdirected.

It's all too easy to send it off on a wild-goose chase, and get it retrieving things that we don't want to be focusing on. It's like a big, soft, daft dog. It doesn't discern between good and bad things. It just does what you tell it to. Why? Well, it doesn't know the difference.

For example, if you constantly assert that you have no time, this data is passed down the information superhighway of your brain to your RAS. 'Ah ha,' it thinks, 'this mum believes she has no time, I'll do my obedient best to prove to her that she's right.' Unless you tell your brain what you want, it will find as much evidence as it possibly can to prove what you are asserting. It searches for evidence that you really do have no time. It encourages you to be late, it encourages you to procrastinate. Like a puppy dog, it just wants to please, and will give you whatever you seem to be asking for.

If you had a badly behaved dog you would take it firmly by the collar and get it to the nearest puppy trainer. Do the same with your grey matter. Get it out of the doghouse. Train your brain.

'Eye Want' Does Get (What Have You Got Your Eye On?)

So how can you harness the horsepower of this fabulous tool to get you more time? It's easy. Just like the Sat Nav or the cabby, get precise with it about what you want. The old adage 'I want doesn't get' does not apply here. Tell your brain what you desire and let it help you get it. Like a new muscle, exercise it and watch it grow as it helps you focus on and get what you want.

Eye Want … Create a Life Shopping List

Look at your desired Eye of Time and think for a moment of all the things that you want to have time for.

Spot the difference:

'I want a tidy house.'	*'I don't want to always be tidying up children's toys.'*
'I want to be on time.'	*'I don't want to be late any more.'*
'I want to take things at a steady pace.'	*'I don't want to rush.'*
'I want to run a half-marathon.'	*'I don't want to feel unfit.'*
'I want to be calm.'	*'I don't want this stress.'*
'I want real quality time with the children.'	*'I don't want to miss out on the children.'*
'I want to spend more time at home.'	*'I don't want to spend so much time at work.'*

Quite often when I ask mums what they want, they will reply by reeling off a long list of what they don't want. The 'I don't want' approach doesn't work for your RAS. It needs to know what you do want. If you have unwanted items turn them into most wanted, by rephrasing them more positively.

From the Mouths of Mums:

What I don't want:

'I'm fed up with running around all day, feeling like I never achieve anything. I don't want this heavy feeling like I've got the world on my shoulders. I don't want to spend all my time clearing up after the kids and picking up their mess. I've lost myself. I don't want to be this crazed woman who runs around and shouts at her children all day long. This isn't the real me. I don't want to be washing up four times a day. I don't want bitten nails. I don't want to just snatch a sandwich at my desk at lunchtime. I don't want to just eat the kids' leftover food at teatime.'

What I do want:

'I want time to relax throughout the day. I'd like to find time to sit down for a cup of coffee at least twice, for 20 minutes every day. By eight o'clock at night I want to feel energized, with all

my jobs complete and the house tidy. Everything will be put away where it belongs, so I can sit and enjoy whatever I choose to do to relax in the evening. I want time to plan our holidays, family outings and a fitness regime. The new me will have a manicure every fortnight. I will eat a proper well-balanced lunch twice a week and on other days buy a sandwich, but take it out and eat it in the park. When I am at home I will eat a proper lunch with the children.'

Knowing what you want will galvanize your RAS into action. Compare Paula and Martha below. It's easy to guess who is likely to get more out of the time they have available.

Perfect Paula's View of Life	**Manic Martha's View of Life**
I'm very clear about what I want to get out of life.	*I know I don't want to be disorganized and unhappy all the time.*
I often think about my goals and how I can achieve them.	*If I get through the day I think I'm doing quite well.*
My life is going where I want it to.	*My life seems to be going nowhere in particular.*
If I had an extra hour every day I know exactly what I would do with it.	*I would love an extra hour every day, but I'm not sure how I'd make it work for me.*

I have a clear picture of what I want from my life.

Something seems to be missing from my life but I'm not quite sure what.

Do you focus on what you want? Read this story to see the possible consequences of misguided focus.

Tip! *When going out to meet a friend, have their phone number to hand so you can ring ahead if you are running late.*

The Two Princesses and the Frog

Once upon a time there was a King who ruled a land far, far away. He had two beautiful daughters, Princess Brea and Princess Isla. His one wish was that they would each find a Prince who would make them happy. Brea knew exactly what she wanted: a tall, dark, handsome Prince with a kind heart and good nature. She wanted someone who shared the same interests as her and had similar values. Isla was clear, too: nobody ugly, no one too bossy, domineering or manipulative. Definitely no one who had different values from her, and please no snorers.

One day the girls were playing with a golden ball by the wishing well in the royal garden. Brea threw the ball to Isla. She missed it and it fell to the bottom of the well. Both girls were distraught, for the golden ball was a gift from their father. As they peered down the well, thinking the ball was gone for ever, they were startled by a croaky voice.

'I can get the ball for you,' it said.

The Princesses looked up and there, sitting in front of them, was a big, green frog.

'Thank you,' said Brea, 'that's so kind of you.'

'On one condition,' the frog added. 'You let me sleep on each of your pillows for three nights.'

'What a manipulative old frog,' said Isla, 'let's tell him to hop off. I don't want an ugly old frog sitting on my pillow.'

'Oh come on, Isla, it's only three nights, and we'll get the ball back. I'll go first if you want.'

So it was that the frog sat on Princess Brea's pillow for the next three nights. The frog and Princess Brea began to talk, and each night Brea got to know the frog a little better. They had many conversations and found they had common views. The frog was good-natured and had a kind heart. Brea told Isla that the frog was kind and she shouldn't worry about having him on her pillow. Isla was adamant that the frog was a slimy old thing with an ulterior motive, and that nobody was bossing her about. For her three nights Isla ignored the frog and refused to look at him.

On the seventh morning, they all went down to the well. The frog, true to his word, retrieved the golden ball. Isla took it somewhat ungraciously. Brea turned to the frog and thanked him. She bent over and gave him a small kiss on the head. In that moment the frog turned into a tall, dark, handsome Prince. Brea and the Prince lived happily ever after. Isla is still searching for her Prince Right. Unfortunately, no matter what she does she still keeps seeing Prince Wrong everywhere she looks.

Are you focusing on what you want or what you don't want? Whichever it is, you'll keep seeing it.

Tip! Carry a plastic zip-bag with you to catch bits of information, receipts, etc. you will want to put away when you get home. Empty it daily.

Put Some Rocket Fuel in Your Tank

If we get what we focus on, why not give your RAS something even clearer to aim for? You've outlined your ideal Eye of Time. Let's take this a step further and do something that will help you get to the land of 'More Time' even faster. Make your destination even more vivid. Imagine you are having a day that reflects what you would like your life to be like. Let's pretend for a moment that you have actually reached your destination. You have more time and you are experiencing your perfect day. This level of clarity will really put rocket fuel in your RAS. Try your perfect day on for size. Do the exercise below.

Exercise – Dream Your Way to Destination 'More Time'

Sit in a comfortable chair. From this chair you are going to become the director of a new blockbuster film called My Perfect Day. Imagine that in front of you is a large screen where you, as director (and star!), are going to preview this fabulous new film. You have total artistic and creative control. When you're ready for the action to begin, in your mind's eye see yourself on the screen. Notice how you are. Who else is there? Notice the sounds. How are you feeling? Make the picture clear, make it large, and make it full colour. Make the sounds audible. Make it a moving film.

Really play around with it – as director you can do whatever you like. Do you want to play the really good bits in slow motion? Bring it closer, move it further away. Keep editing until this really is fabulous and you feel fantastic watching it. Now imagine that you're not just watching yourself from the chair, you're really in the film. You are experiencing everything that the 'you' on the screen is experiencing, hearing what she's hearing and seeing what she's seeing. Enjoy this movie until you're ready to come back to the director's chair.

Isn't it fantastic, seeing yourself living a day when you have enough time to do what you want? My guess is that what you were viewing wasn't a day that was cluttered and full of urgency. It was one that reflected your desired Eye of Time. Do this every day as many times as you like, having fun with the images. Do it in the bath, on the bus, when you're bored, in a meeting. Do it whenever you can.

You're training your brain to expect the perfect day. By knowing what you want and by starting to focus on it, it will begin to appear in your life. You already know how to create a Magic Hour to do the things of your choosing. How much more time could you create to enjoy your perfect day if you put your mind to it?

What Do You Want to Do Before You Die?

Why not take this a step further? What do you want to fit into the rest of your life? A bit of a morose question, I know. Most of us are ecstatic if we can galvanize our brain cells into thinking to the end of next week, let alone the end of our lives. Mums have a lot of catching up when it comes to doing what we want with our time. But it's far better to think about it now than later, when it might just be too late.

Exercise – The End of Your Fabulous Life

Imagine for a moment that you are an old lady at the end of your life. Think about these questions:

What do my children say about me?

What do my family and friends say about me?

What are the highlights of my life?

What are my major achievements?

How much have I enjoyed my life?

If I had more time what would I still want to do?

Is there anything missing from my life?

The things that made my life rich and varied were ...

Are the answers to these questions what you want to hear? If not, start thinking about what you want to do with all the gold dust you've got left in your egg timer, not just the immediate day ahead.

If you want to get really focused, try writing your own obituary. That's a pretty sobering way to get you thinking about how you're spending your time.

Tip! *Clean the shower after each use with a car squeegee – stops the build-up of limescale and saves cleaning time.*

From the Mouths of Kids:

'Mummy was always really busy doing something, mostly the washing up, or nagging at me. She never seemed to have any time to play. She seemed cross a lot of the time.'

The Long-term View from the Eye of Time

If you take the Life Focus categories from your Eye of Time, think what you would want to achieve in each of them over the next 20 years. What do you want to achieve in your career, friendships, health and financial life? Recognize that although you will always be a mum, your children will grow and change. At each stage of their growth they will make differing demands on your time. How can you manage your life and set goals that reflect these changes in their needs, while still meeting your own? You can become so bogged down as you race from the toddler to teen years, that you forget there might be light at the end of the tunnel when they leave home. For once, it might even be light, rather than a train coming in the other direction! Will you know what you want to do?

Make a list of everything you want to achieve in your life. Use the Dream-Catcher on page 102 as a prompt, to get you thinking about long-term and short-term goals in every area of your life. Write down everything you can think of: new hobbies, friends you want to see, holidays you want to have, places you'd like to visit, projects you'd like to start, health achievements, people you'd love to meet. Anything from any aspect of your life; collect it all up. Crazy as it may seem, the more goals you have, the more you will achieve. If you only write down two things, like 'go to Disneyland' and 'visit Belinda in Sydney', they're very likely to happen. A hundred per cent success, well done you. What if you write down 100 things and only get 50 per cent? Think how much more you'll have achieved! If you achieve all your goals in life, then my guess is you don't have enough goals.

Tip! Look for examples of when you've managed your time well. Ask your brain to focus on these, and seek opportunities to use the same strategies again.

From the Mouths of Mums:

'I really want to go back to work. The children are all at secondary school. The problem is, I've never really thought about this until now and now I feel like it's a bit late. I wish I'd had it in my mind a few years ago.'

My Dream-Catcher

	1 month	3 months	6 months	1 year	5 years	10 years	20 years
Career							
Fun/leisure							
Family							
Friendships							
Physical							
Environment							
Romance/ partner							
Money							
Health							

Tip! Keep a list of things that can be done in fewer than ten minutes. Whenever you have just ten minutes, do one of them.

'PEP' Up Your Long-term Life Focus

Take all the dreams you've written on your Dream-Catcher and turn them into goals. You're going to write them in such a way that it will make it much easier for your RAS to seek them out with the power of a guided missile. We're going to use the PEP approach to goal setting: Make your goals **P**ositive, **E**xplicit and **P**resent.

Positive Goals

Make your goals a positive statement of what you want, rather than what you *don't* want.
For example:

'I want to feel and look like a sex goddess.'
vs
'I don't want to look like a sack of old potatoes.'

'I want to spend at least 30 minutes, one-on-one real quality time with each of my children every day.'
vs
'I don't want to run round like a headless chicken, wondering when I will have time to play with my children.'

Explicit Goals

Be as detailed as possible about your goal. Write down as much evidence as you can that will let you know you've achieved it. For example, if one of your goals is to take salsa lessons, how will you know you've achieved it? You could say, 'Well, I'll be taking salsa lessons,' it's obvious. However, you could give yourself more detail. Think about questions like:

When will you have them?
How often will you have them?
Whom will you be with?

Paint a picture in your mind of you achieving the goal. What do you see, hear and feel? For example:

'It's the summer, and every second Wednesday I go salsa dancing with Chris.'
vs
'I go salsa dancing.'

'I've just finished my first half-marathon. I'm 35, and the crowd is cheering as I cross the finishing line.'
vs
'I'm running a half-marathon.'

Present Goals

Write your goal in the present tense as if you have already achieved it. Even if the goal is 20 years off, avoid vague, future-based constructions:

'I am having a facial every six weeks at the really nice salon in town.'
vs
'Someday in the next ten years when I have time I will have a facial every six weeks.'

Some more examples of present goals:

'People are buying my paintings.'
'Someone else is doing the ironing.'
'I'm 64 years old, I have three grandchildren and they think I'm the best granny in the world.'
'I'm on safari with the children.'
'The extension on the house is finished and I love it.'
'I have an au pair to help me.'

Now you've PEPed up your goals, you'll want to know how to start turning them into reality. That's exactly what we'll be doing next week, but to do that you need to create a Destiny Diary.

Creating a Destiny Diary

A Destiny Diary is the home for your PEP Goals. It's the foundation stone in the formation and manifestation of your fabulous future. In true *Blue Peter* style, to make yours you will need:

- A ring binder
- Paper
- Pens
- Section-divider cards

1. Create seven sections in your Destiny Diary.
The first section holds PEP Goals for the next month, the second section for the next three months, the third for the next six months, and so on. Put in seven sections to hold PEP Goals for the next 20 years. (Feel free to plan further if you want!)

2. In each section have eight sheets of paper headed with one of your Life Focus Categories: Career, Fun/leisure, Family, Friendships, Physical Environment, Romance/partner, Money, Health.

3. On the top left-hand side of the page write 'PEP Goal' and on the top right-hand side write 'Destiny Date'.

4. Write your PEPed-up Goals on the relevant Life Focus sheet in the relevant time section. Make sure you give each PEP Goal a Destiny Date. That is the date you want to achieve it by. For example, 'It is my 35th birthday and I am running a half-marathon.' Would be written on the Health page in the section for next year. If this seems like a big task to do in one go, try time-chunking. Break the task down into small pieces and tackle a little bit at a time. So, instead of spending a couple of hours on this, spend 15 minutes a day transferring PEP Goals until it's done. In the next chapter you'll learn how to take these PEP Goals and turn them into reality.

Be the Architect of Your Own Destiny

You are the architect of your own destiny. Like any good architect, you need a vision. You absolutely have to know what the focus of your efforts is going to be in order to turn that vision into reality. Just like a jigsaw puzzle, you need an image to guide you as you build the picture of your life. In the next two chapters we'll learn fabulous techniques around planning and organizing. These will help you to bring the things that you want to focus on into your near vision. Not just the perfect day. I'm thinking more along the lines of the perfect life. In Chapter 4 you'll learn how to develop a system which will allow you to get it all done and still have time to achieve the PEPed-up dreams and goals you've just created.

Actions for Week Three

- Look at your ideal Eye of Time for a minute every day. (one minute)
- When you brush your teeth each morning, set your intent to have a great day, in which everything gets done. (two minutes)
- Each night, review your day. Ask yourself the question, 'Where did I waste time and where could I have saved it?' (two minutes)
- Watch your personal film, My Perfect Day, three times this week. (five minutes is fine, but do it for longer if you wish)
- Create a Destiny Diary and fill it with PEP Goals. (one hour 45 minutes or 15 minutes every day for a week)
- Do one thing towards one of your long-term PEP Goals. However small, choose to make time to take a step forward. It might be a phone call or buying a book, just do something. (ten minutes)

Summary

- Like a shopping basket without a list, your day will fill up with whatever drops into it, unless you choose what to put in it.
- Unless you know what you want to do with your time, you'll never find time to do it.
- Make a decision about what you choose to do with your time, not what you don't choose to do.

- When you focus on what you want in life, you tend to get more of it.
- Use your Eye of Time, Life Focus Eye and Values Focus Eye to plot out what you want to focus on.
- People who write down what they want to achieve get more done.
- Your Reticular Activating System (RAS) can help you get more of what you want in life.
- It's useful to mentally rehearse having more time.
- Create a Destiny Diary to capture everything you want to have time to do in the weeks, months and years ahead.

Week Four

Become the Mistress of Your Own Time

An Ode to Plans

I've got snot on my skirt, and sick on my shirt,
Everything's covered in kiddie dessert,
I've no time to change,
So I'll just look deranged,
In clothes smeared with baby food,
Thrown from close range.
What I really want now is a sleep or long soak,
But no time, I'll have to drink coffee and coke,
I've lost control, it just is no joke,
Life would be easy if I were a bloke.
I've no time to eat, that would just be a treat,
A romantic meal an impossible feat.
Real food would be great,
But it's part of mums' fate,
To only eat scraps the kids leave on their plate.
Where is that note I wrote to myself?
I'm sure it was there, in that pile on the shelf,
When was the party for Lucy and Fay?
Oh bugger, it happened yesterday,
I'll have to ring them or send them a note,
If it goes on like this I'll cut my own throat.
I've got so much to do, it makes me feel blue,
And where should I start? I haven't a clue.
My list is so long,
Where do I go wrong?
I need a plan to move me along.

Time Truths 1 2 3 4 5 6 7

Take control of time or time will take control of you

Turning Your Dreams and To-dos into Reality

'Look after the minutes and the hours will look after themselves.'

Well done, you are now the proud owner of the most elongated list of goals, dreams and aspirations you've probably ever seen in your life. How on earth do you turn this work of fiction into your autobiography? A fantastic and fascinating story of your life. Knowing what you want to focus on is a fabulous step forward.

Now comes the greatest challenge: finding time to fit it all in, time to squeeze every last drop of time from every day. In this chapter you'll learn the secrets of successful planning. With a plan you can bring your goals and aspirations into your near focus and take action to make them a reality. You'll learn how to prioritize your life to get things done. Your RAS is revved up and ready to go.

What you have to do now is grab hold of the steering wheel and get moving. If you're a Perfect Paula you'll know the secrets of planning. If, on the other hand, you're more of a Manic Martha, this chapter is absolutely for you.

Think about yourself. How effective are you at taking positive action to get yourself what you want from your time? Do you feel more like a lump of lard than a Time Lord when it comes to the question of galvanizing yourself into action? Look at the statements opposite to see how much you really need this chapter to get you on your way.

Tip! If you are taking small children swimming first thing in the morning, take them in their pyjamas and get them dressed after their swim. If you are taking them at the end of the day, get them ready for bed before bringing them home.

Something to think about ...

	Agree	Disagree	Partly agree
I get the things done each day that are really important to me.	❑	❑	❑
I have one diary where I keep track of everything.	❑	❑	❑
I spend a little bit of time each day planning my day.	❑	❑	❑
I have a note of all the things I need to do and I know they will get done.	❑	❑	❑
I know how to cope when things come up that prevent me from doing what I set out to.	❑	❑	❑
I always know which job to tackle first.	❑	❑	❑
I manage to get high-value, important things done each day.	❑	❑	❑
When I make a plan I can easily focus on it.	❑	❑	❑
I have a strategy for getting all my tasks done.	❑	❑	❑
I always turn up on time to events with everything I need.	❑	❑	❑

If you answered mostly 'Agree', well done you! You've got top marks. If on the other hand you answered mostly 'Disagree' and/or 'Partly agree', proceed directly to the next paragraph. Do not pass go. Do not collect £200. Do not stop reading until you've got the essence of this chapter well and truly ingrained in your brain. You are going to learn how to sort the wheat from the chaff, take action in a way that will enable you to get everything done, and free up your time so you can propel yourself at light speed towards any goal you choose to pursue.

Help, Where Do I Start?

If you're like every other mother on this planet, your average To-do List is likely to be as long as your leg, as depressing as cellulite and, like the bags under your eyes, just keeps on getting bigger. Into the bargain you've just added a whole new list of things you want to achieve over the next 20 years. Unless you've got some way of dealing with all of this, life can seem totally overwhelming. It's a bit like swimming in porridge, or wading through treacle. A highly unpleasant way to live.

You've tried it, it bogs you down and it makes you stressed. Why keep doing it? Why not try something different? I have a very interesting theory, a new method for you to try. It's called the *Wine Bottle Theory of Time Management*. You may be wondering what a bottle of wine could possibly have to do with time management. You may not even really care, but the mere mention of wine has caused you to perk up and take notice!

Now, before you get too excited and trip over your own feet, randomly abandoned toys and the cat as you dash excitedly towards the wine rack, I have to state very clearly that this approach is not a licence to drink gallons of Chilean Chardonnay. I repeat, this is not a licence to drink gallons of Chilean Chardonnay as a way out of your time-management mayhem. (Although I have been told a few glasses of this happy water have been known to numb the pain, I wouldn't know myself.)

The Wine Bottle Theory of Time Management

Whatever your thoughts, it's a serious theory. Follow the wisdom of this method and I guarantee it will revolutionize your day. Never again will you be at a loss when you look at your loathsome life full of lists of things you need to do. For the first time ever, when faced with what seems like an insurmountable number of tasks and chores, using the techniques from this theory you'll be able to decipher where to start and what to do first. Then you'll feel great because you've made an inroad.

Yes, you will make a dent in what needs to be done. You will be moving from reactivity to proactivity. Having no time will be a thing of the past. The humble wine bottle will be your oracle (what do you mean, it already is?). Your PEP Goals will be transformed into actionable items, which you will get done. I know you can't believe it, but get the hang of the wine bottle method and you'll be swinging from the lampshade, singing for joy.

Gathering the Ingredients

So what does one need to get their wits around this? Well, for ease of understanding I will break the theory down into a few digestible morsels, so that you can instantly understand and begin to get the benefits. I'll make it as simple to follow as possible. Unlike many other learned theories, you won't choke as you try to swallow this one.

Tip! *Take yourself off junk-mail lists.*

Step One

As with any great recipe for success, you need to assemble a few key ingredients:

- A wine carafe (if, like me, you're not that posh and don't have one, worry not, a plastic jug will do)
- An open bottle of wine (tricky I know, but full of wine, please)
- A bag of apples
- A carton of blueberries
- A bag of caster sugar

An odd mêlée of ingredients, I agree, but just you wait and see what magic we're going to do with them. These ingredients symbolize your day.

Imagine that your day is the jug. All the empty space in it represents the hours, minutes and seconds of your day. On any given day you will endeavour to get as many tasks done as possible. So the object of the exercise is to squeeze as much as you can into the jug.

The apples, blueberries, caster sugar and wine represent all the tasks you have to do. Your challenge is to fill the jug to the brim with them. Faced with an empty jug, how do you get the maximum amount in? What do you put in first, the apples, blueberries, caster sugar or wine? Progress to step two and you'll find out.

Step Two

Put as many apples as you can into the jug so it's full to the top with just apples and there is no room for any more. The jug is full – or is it?

Step Three

Put as many blueberries as you can in the jug. They should fit in around the apples, filling up the smaller gaps. Do this until the jug looks full and there is no room for any more blue-berries. The jug is full – or is it?

Step Four

Take the caster sugar and pour in as much as you can, until, once again, the jug looks full and there is no room for any more. The jug is completely and utterly full to the top – or is it?

Step Five

Although it really will look full now, don't be deceived.

Take your bottle of wine and pour some in. As you do this, remember this experiment is in the interests of science, your sanity and personal development. Try not to think too much about the fact that you could actually be drinking the stuff rather than pouring it over the apples, blueberries and sugar! Unbelievably, as it trickles into the jug there will still be some very small spaces that the liquid is able to fill. You may even be surprised by how much wine the jug is able to take (like you after a hard day at work or being driven mad by the kids!). Keep going until the jug is full to capacity and to get any more in you would need another jug, or a new day.

Tip! *Work out in which part of the day you are at your best, and plan your work accordingly.*

Step Six

Stand back and look in amazement at how much you've been able to fit easily into the jug. Avoid thinking about what a horrible sticky mess it's going to be to clean up, just look on in wonderment.

Step Seven

Ponder for a moment how this little exercise might revolutionize your life. For most of us, the jug that represents our day gets too full, too quickly. We often find ourselves at the end of the day with a pile of leftover ingredients sitting next to the jug. Without exception I find this to be the case. Whether you're a working mum or a stay-at-home mum, the complaint is always the same: my jug gets too full, too quickly with things that aren't what I really want. Why is this?

Well, you don't need a degree in rocket science to realize that what we did here was put the big things in first and then the progressively smaller and smaller things, until the jug was filled to the top. To get the maximum amount into your jug, you must start with the apples. Do it any other way and you get fewer apples in or no apples at all. But 'Why?', I hear you cry. 'Why put the apples in first?'

Apples First

The apples in your jug represent the most important things that you have to do in your day. If you don't do these, then your world will fall apart. They have to be tackled right there and then. Your tax return has to be in tomorrow or you'll be fined. This would be an apple.

Tip! *Always add buffer time: plan to be there with time to spare.*

Bring on Your Blueberries Second

The blueberries represent the tasks that are your lesser priorities that day. These can fit in around the apples.

They're the items that you want to appear in your near focus, but you always endeavour to find a way of tackling your apple tasks first.

From the Mouths of Mums:

'Reading a story to my little girl every night before she goes to sleep appears every day on my "Action List" as an activity I want to complete. When you work full time it's all too easy to let work slip into your focus and the kids get kind of fuzzy in your peripheral vision. Letting a meeting overrun, taking that extra phone call or just looking at those e-mails one last time might be the things that tip the balance and stop me getting home in time to read the bedtime story. Now I've committed to making this part of my daily routine. People know not to ask me if I'll do things at the last minute. They know I'll be leaving work on time. It's only since I've done all this work on Choice and Focus that I've realized actually it's my choice whether I stay at work or come home. Knowing time with my children is high up on my priority list helps me make the right choice about what to do. And guess what? That time is so magical I wouldn't swap it for anything. I feel great because I'm focusing on something that's of great value to me.'

Don't Get Caught Up with Caster Sugar

The caster sugar represents those tasks that you want in your far focus until you are ready to do them, i.e. when you've done the more important things. I think here of things like social telephone calls.

Be a Wine-NO

Wine represents the most low-grade tasks you have on your list, the fluff, the filler, the things you do only when everything else has been completed. If you're like me, given the choice of an apple, a blueberry, a spoonful of sugar or a bottle of wine, there's no competition. I'll go for the wine every time. So often we do this in life.

When faced with a series of options, we go for the one that instantly gratifies us rather than the one that doesn't instantly appeal but provides us with a longer-term benefit. Faced with the choice of pain or pleasure, we choose pleasure. Well, come on, we are human. This is the danger in our lives. We tackle the vino first. We fill our jug to the brim with wine, and leave no room for the apples and the blueberries. When your jug is full of apples it's always possible to add some wine. When your jug is full of wine, it's not possible to add anything. The apples, blueberries and caster sugar remain untouched on the counter, at the side of the jug. They remain on your list of things to do, day after day. Sober up, put the wine down, and be a wine-NO.

What Makes Your Apples, Blueberries, Caster Sugar and Wine?

Now you know how to fill your jug to maximum capacity, all that remains is to ascertain what, in your life, makes up your apples, blueberries, sugar and wine. To help you decide, I present for your ease of selection a fabulous decision-making matrix. If you're like me, you'll want to make it simple. I know, after a long day at work, or an afternoon with the kids, I am totally unable to cope with a complicated concept like a decision-making matrix. So, to save us from brain ache and to continue our pleasant retail theme, we will be adopting the shopping-basket method of decision making. Let's shop till we drop, ladies.

As we already know, most mums just toss their groceries randomly into their basket, in the same haphazard way that they approach their lives. You, however, are not like other mums. You approach your shopping in a much more organized fashion, with a list.

Imagine for a moment that your basket only has four compartments, and today you are shopping for only four items. Yes, you've guessed it – today you're shopping for apples, blueberries, caster sugar and wine.

Which compartment of your basket you place these goods in will depend very much on how urgently you really need them, and on how valuable they are to your life. Take a look at the shopping basket opposite to get to grips with what we're talking about.

Life Value

The right and left-hand sides of the basket represent value to your life. The further up the basket an item is placed, the more valuable it is to you. Conversely, the nearer to the bottom of the basket an item is placed, the less valuable it is. At the bottom of the basket items with low value are placed; towards the top of the basket more valuable items are placed (the ones you don't want to get squashed). Squashed blueberries just drive

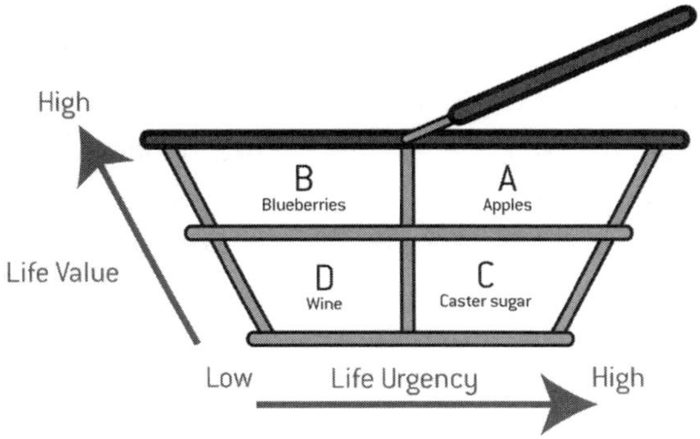

The Shopping Basket of Life

you mad, don't they? And you know what happens if you put your heavy bottle of wine on top of your delicate apples – you end up with a basket full of bashed, bruised and horrible-tasting fruit.

Life Urgency

The urgency of the item, or how quickly you might want to put it into your jug of life when you get home, is represented by the parallel lines at the top and bottom of the basket. The left-hand side of the basket represents low-urgency products, and the right-hand side of the basket represents high-urgency products.

Life value and life urgency are two quite different things, as this mum demonstrates.

From the Mouths of Mums:

'When I was 36 years old I was diagnosed with ovarian cancer. I was devastated. It certainly

made me re-evaluate my priorities, and time took on a different meaning. My illness gave me clarity of vision that allowed me to see what was really of value in my life: my husband, my children and my health. I realized that until this bolt of lightning struck me, I'd not been living my life in a way that reflected this. I was always putting the children to one side, telling them to hang on because I was busy doing other things, none of them terribly important, although they seemed so at the time. Suddenly the value I put on each day, each moment, became different. I'm in remission now and things look positive, but when your own mortality looks you in the face you suddenly realize what actually is of value to you, and it's not necessarily the things that seemed "urgent" before.'

We select and place items in our basket based on how valuable they are and how urgent they are. When we know their relative urgency and value we can prioritize more easily, deciding what to do first.

A Is for Apple – Near Focus

In the top right-hand corner we put shopping that represents the most valuable and most urgent things to be done in our world. In other words, our apples. These are our number-one, or A, priorities, the things we will tackle first. Sometimes these are items we have no control over. Life happens. George gets a piece of Lego stuck up his nose and has to be rushed to the Accident and Emergency department to have it removed. This is an urgent and important task. Other times we do have control over how many apples we have in our daily basket. You've chosen to leave making up Natalie's lunch box until the last minute. She has to have her lunch, you're about to leave for school. This now becomes an urgent and valuable activity. It has to be undertaken there and then.

This is how you end up living in reaction. Apples have to be done, but try to prevent them building up in your basket. If you've too many apples in your cart, it only takes one to go rotten and life can start getting a bit stressful. If you want to keep the doctor away, try just one apple a day, or even better, stick to blueberries.

B Is for Blueberries – Medium Focus

In the top left-hand corner we put shopping that represents high-value, low-urgency items. These tasks are represented by the blueberries in our basket. They are your number-two, or B, priorities. Because they aren't urgent these are the tasks that we often put off. Do so at your peril, as they invariably come back to bite you on the bum at a later date. Like a time-bomb waiting to explode in your face, don't deal with these and you're asking for trouble. Their seeming lack of urgency will lure you into a false sense of security, allowing you to believe that they can be pushed into peripheral vision and left for another day. But you know how it is, another day never comes. Until of course you've left them for so long they morph into the monster of all apples, becoming valuable and ultra-urgent.

Tip! *Always look at the label before you buy anything. Is it going to be tricky to wash or iron?*

From the Mouths of Mums:

'I'd known for six months that I had to get my son's passport updated, I just kept putting off going to the Post Office because I knew how long the queue would be. In the end I put it off so long I ended up having to go to the embassy and queue nearly all day. What was I thinking of? Why didn't I just do it when it was a blueberry instead of letting it turn into an apple?'

By tackling blueberry tasks as a priority when they are not urgent, it prevents them from ever moving into the apple category. Being proactive about doing these tasks saves you from the stress of living in reaction and having to fire-fight at a later date.

Children, Your Biggest Blueberries

A fabulous example of something that falls into this category is time with your children. For most of us our precious angels are undoubtedly the most highly valued things in our lives. Yet how many of us believe that we don't spend as much time with them as we want to? In Legal & General's 2004 'Value of a Mum' survey, more than half of the 500 respondents said they didn't spend enough time together as a family. This rose to 61 per cent for full-time workers. Sadly, family falls into the 'blueberry category': valuable, but not urgent.

As a parent coach I regularly speak to mums who tell me their children are badly behaved. More often than not, bad behaviour can be put down to attention-seeking. Children turn themselves into urgencies so you pay attention to them. They jump up and down, have tantrums, bite and squabble. You know the routine, I'm sure. They do this just to get some of your time. It's a sad state of affairs.

Many of us only spend time paying attention to our children when they turn themselves into highly important and highly urgent items. They make us deal with them by behaving badly. By recognizing our children as valuable and giving time to them when it's needed, not just when it becomes urgent, we can live our lives in a less stressful way.

From the Mouths of Mums:

'I know this sounds crazy, but when I started to timetable quality time in my diary for playing with my children, and I really focused on them and what they wanted to do without any distractions, their behaviour generally improved. It was amazing.'

'When my youngest was only one, I realized that my health and vitality were really important and valuable to me. With a small child I just never

got time to exercise. Keeping fit was a blueberry task for me. I knew it was valuable, but it wasn't urgent and I wasn't focusing any attention on it at all. I told myself that I didn't have time to do it. Exercise was well and truly in my peripheral vision. When I got the concept of valuable and urgent tasks, I decided that I had to do something about it, because not feeling fit and healthy was also affecting how I felt about myself. So I got creative. I booked a personal trainer who came to my house once a week and I invested in an exercise bike. I used it when the children were in bed. That way I had a chance of getting my blueberries done! I cycled and watched TV – blueberries and wine at the same time, what a result! I made it easier for myself to succeed.'

The Benefits of Blueberries

The benefits of focusing on as many blueberries as you can are huge. We all know an apple a day keeps the doctor away, but I think that saying was coined before we really knew about the secret properties of the blueberry.

Often cited as a 'super food', you want to be consuming as many of these in a day as you can. Tackle these and for once you'll be doing the most important things in your life first. By 'most important things' I mean the actions that will move you towards the goals you defined in the last chapter. The things you said you wanted to be focusing time and energy on. If you were getting those things done by tackling a handful of blueberries a day, just think how you would feel.

If you found the time to take some small steps last week towards achieving your goals, you'll already have a sense of how that makes you feel: fantastic. Why is Perfect Paula always on top of life? She's got the valuable but non-urgent things sorted. She's chosen to focus on them and get them done. Non-urgent but important tasks have a way of creeping up on you if you don't deal with them early on. The moral of this tale: get your apples out of the way, then quickly crack on with your blueberries.

Like all fruit, left in the basket for too long they'll start to go mouldy. Blueberries, particularly, have a nasty habit of catching up with you if you neglect them. As an advertisement in my local sports centre read: *'There's no such thing as a sudden heart attack.'*

Make sure you're attending to your blueberries as a priority, before they become your urgencies.

Tip! *Jot down ideas on paper or in a journal – don't rely on your memory.*

C Is for Caster Sugar – Far Focus

In the bottom right-hand corner, we put shopping that represents low-value, high-urgency items. These tasks are represented by the caster sugar in our basket. These are our number-three, or C, priorities. They should stay in our far focus until all our As and Bs are complete. Often we are tempted to bring these tasks into our near focus first, because they are urgent. They demand our attention.

Often they are easy to do, so very tempting to tackle. The telephone is always a classic in this regard. How much time did you waste on the phone last week? Just because it rings, we think we must answer it. We don't know if it's of value until we pick it up. What if it's a double-glazing salesman?

From the Mouths of Mums:

'Before I understood about planning I used to think that the most important thing in my life was keeping the house clean. Doing this hasn't changed my view on the fact that I want a clean house, but this is no longer an obsession of mine. By employing a cleaner for a couple of hours a week and farming out some of the chores to the kids, I've minimized the amount of time I now have to spend on cleaning. I try to think of cleaning as a caster-sugar task, not an apple task. I was a bit sceptical at first, but I've been amazed at how I can keep the house clean and free up time for me to do other stuff. I've got a little part-time job in the local post office, which to be honest I really needed. Being at home all day was driving me crazy.

It pays for the cleaner, I enjoy work and my children are becoming more responsible as they do their chores. I actually feel like a better role model. I get more done and I have more time.'

D is for Wine – Peripheral Vision

In the bottom left-hand corner we put shopping that represents low-value, low-urgency items. These should be in our peripheral vision, only coming into near focus when all other tasks have been tackled. These tasks are represented by the wine in our basket. They are your number-four, or D, priorities. Quite frankly, these are the things that would make no difference whatsoever to our lives if we didn't do them. Things like, 'I'll just call Jackie even though I spoke to her in the school playground only 20 minutes ago.'

Like wine, these appealing tasks tend to lure you towards them temptingly. They distract you from focusing on your higher priorities. You know the kinds of things I mean: staying on the phone too long, clearing out your purse, wiping the surface of the kitchen even though it's not dirty, or watching a film that you've seen before. Now I'm not saying any of these things are wrong. You might even decide that you really do want to watch that film again.

The difference comes when you consciously choose to do it, rather than just falling into it as an activity at the expense of things that you value more and are more urgent in your life.

On the whole, D priorities are things that just catch our attention. I have a terrible habit of reading the property section of my local paper. We're not moving house and we're not selling our house, it's not important and it's not urgent, so why on earth do I do it?

Tip! *Use washing tablets – no measuring required.*

Tip! *Invest 12 minutes every day working out what you want to achieve tomorrow.*

From the Mouths of Mums:

'When I looked at what I was placing in my jug, I decided that it must look like I was an alcoholic, the amount of wine I was pouring in, or in my case coffee. For me coffee is an essential part of life. I can't do without it, and I realized that I planned regular trips to the coffee machine down the hallway, which always turned into a ten-minute chat with a colleague. Now, it's important for me to network and mingle. It's part of my job to know what's going on, but if I was truthful with myself I didn't need to be trotting off down there five times a day. It was a wine activity. So I started to focus on apple and blueberry tasks. I only allowed myself to get a coffee if I completed them. The coffee trip was like a reward. I started to notice that I became much more productive.'

Value + Urgency = Priority

Knowing the value and urgency of any item in your life will enable you to decide its relative priority. High-value items are those things that we do because they make a huge difference to our life and will most probably reflect the things we value most. Flick back to your Life Focus and Values Focus Eyes, to remind yourself of what your highest life values are. Sometimes things can be really valuable and important to us, but we don't choose to do them. Why? More often than not there is no sense of urgency associated with them. When things become urgent we're more likely to focus on them, whether or not they hold any value in our lives.

For many people exercise is a high-value activity. Unfortunately, it never gets done because a choice is made to do something more pressing instead. Exercise is easy to put off. We can always do it tomorrow. We move it to our peripheral vision and do something else, like answering the telephone or watching the telly. These activities make themselves urgent by demanding our immediate attention. They talk to us, they ring in our ears or they jump up and down until we attend to them. What are the chances of the exercise bike jumping up and down, demanding that you get on it and work out? In most houses it sits quietly in the corner, gathering dust.

In Short

When you understand the Wine Bottle Theory, you can decide what to bring into your near focus first. It helps you decide where things will sit on your Eye of

Time at any given moment. Your Eye of Time is a dynamic tool.

When you look at Manic Martha's Eye, it usually has wine and caster sugar tasks in its near focus, broken up by apple emergency tasks. With no plan, more important items, like blueberries, tend to sit in peripheral vision, never coming into near focus. This is Paula's skill: she is able to prioritize and plan effectively so items come in and out of her near focus.

When you begin to take control over the traffic coming in and out of your near focus, you too will start to feel more in control of your life. In short, by using the Wine Bottle and Shopping Basket methods you will always know what to tackle first when faced with a million things to do. You can choose what to put in your near focus, your far focus, your peripheral vision and your blind spot. You'll be calling the shots.

The Importance of a Daily Diary and a Destiny Diary

All you need now is a method for capturing and keeping track of everything that has to be done. For this we need two things:

- a Daily Diary
- a Destiny Diary.

Now, I know there are people out there who feel they have no need of a diary. I've met them. I've even met clients who don't wear a watch. 'I can carry it all around in my head,' they declare triumphantly. Given that the average conscious mind can hold only between five and seven pieces of information at any one time, I've yet to meet the human being using this strategy who's getting everything done, and not letting things slip through the cracks of life.

So, unless you are the Bionic Woman, Stephen Hawking or you only have a couple of things to do, you need a diary. Mental Post-it notes just don't hit the mark as a time-management strategy. A planner or diary is as crucial to time management as water is to fish. As for a watch – well, what can I say? Get one right now, you wicked woman.

Get a Daily Diary Today

You don't need to spend a huge amount of your hard-earned cash on a fancy planner. It can be electronic or paper-based, but you do need a diary with enough space to put a list of your tasks each day and to write a few notes in it. Ideally it will have enough space to keep track of the schedules of your whole family.

The Destiny Diary you made last week is also crucial if you want to start finding time to fit in all your longer-term goals. I have a planner that incorporates the two diaries, and I carry it with me at all times. With these two tools at your fingertips you can become the conductor of the orchestra that is your life.

A Typical To-do List

A 'to-do list' is the classic tool for keeping track of all your tasks. The problem is, most of them don't work.

More often than not, people just don't know what to tackle first. Like the Magic Porridge Pot, to-do lists produce an overflowing, never-ending sticky stream of tasks that could easily consume a whole town, let alone one desperate mother. The techniques you've learned around prioritizing will enable you to cut through to-do mountains like a machete through butter.

If your current list looks like an overcrowded house, with uninvited guests, live-in limpets and squatters that you just can't get rid of, here's how you evict them all.

Let's turn your mêlée of to-dos into an 'Action List' that works. Get ready, because what you're about to do will cleanse your soul.

An Action List that Works

We are going to get a definitive list of what you need to get done. On a blank piece of paper, write the heading 'Master List', then get ready to have a 'cerebral dump'.

Write down all the things that you want to do, need to do, and have to do, right now. Really enjoy getting it onto one piece of paper, and don't stop until it's done. Note all the things that have been taking up vital and much-needed space in your brain. Capture everything – the things written on Post-it notes stuck to your fridge, the list in your diary, the list in your notebook, the odd scraps of paper lying around the house, in your purse and in coat pockets. Gather them all up, like lost sheep requiring a pen. Like sheep, your to-dos need somewhere to go where you can account for them all. Then you can decide what to do with them. When you've done this, notice how good it feels to have everything in one place.

The Master List

A typical brain dump might look something like this:

- *Catch up with the ironing*
- *Get Jack and Sam's hair cut*
- *Call the telephone company about the phone bill*
- *Sew the hem on Jack's school trousers*
- *Tidy up every room in the house – they are all a mess*
- *Sort kids' cupboards in their rooms*
- *Get Sam some new school shoes*
- *Learn how to shoot and send videos on my phone*
- *Call Belinda in Australia*
- *Choose material and order curtains for the bathroom*
- *Get leak fixed on kitchen tap – drives me mad!*
- *Get my roots done – look like the wild woman of Borneo*
- *Buy orange hair dye*
- *Buy verucca cream*
- *Order book about interior design*
- *Read my book*
- *Find a cleaner*
- *Take Paul's trousers to the dry cleaners*
- *Disinfect the bin*
- *Buy a new freezer*
- *Watch my favourite TV programme*
- *Have a coffee with Jackie.*

This Master List represents our daily to-dos. We'll come onto our bigger goals later. For those of you who have a job outside the house as well, it'll be scattered with work-related to-dos, too. On the whole, these lists are long and, given the jug of our day, there is just too much to tackle in 24 hours. But having them all in one place lets you look at them in a controlled, calm and objective way, allowing you to decide what to do with them. This will give you a greater sense of control.

Here we have another important key to time management: the ability to choose which thing you will do first, and when you will do everything else. This is what will take you from chaos to control.

Tip! Make a job-lot of sandwiches and put them in the freezer for packed lunches.

Making Mincemeat of Your Master List

Take each task on your Master List in turn and shepherd it to its correct home. This home will be a place in your Daily Diary. Here's how you do it. For each item on your list, ask yourself the following question:

- Is this something I can do today?

If it is, write the task in today's Daily Diary page.
If it's not, ask yourself:

- If I can't do it today, when would it make sense to do this?

Write the task on the appropriate day in your Daily Diary.

Once you've distributed your to-dos around your diary, you can close it and cross the tasks off your Master List. You can now forget about these. (Rest assured – when you need them to they will reappear as if by magic.)

Now, instead of being overwhelmed by a huge list, you can bring specific tasks into your near focus only on the day you have chosen to do them. You can now safely throw away the Master List and all the scraps of paper. If dry cleaning has been assigned to next Wednesday, you can forget about it until then. Like a rabbit out of a hat, it will appear automatically when you open your diary on Wednesday.

> **Tip!** *Always have a Plan B – especially when it comes to childcare arrangements.*

Keeping on Top of Your Action List

This system is foolproof if, of course, you do one crucial thing. You must remember to *open your diary each day* and take a look at what you planned to do. This brings us to a critical point: the issue of planning each day before it happens. This is the key to keeping on top of your 'Actions'. Lamenting the fact that Paul's trousers have still got a big blob of strawberry jam on them and can't be worn to the christening as planned, because you forgot to open your diary on Wednesday and take them to the dry cleaners, is just no good. To ensure that this doesn't happen, at the beginning or end of each day, sit down with your Daily Diary and plan for the day ahead.

Personally I prefer to do it the night before, because I feel more in control when it's done and, quite frankly, in my house you never know what might kick off in the morning. The hamster's great escape in the night is one recent scenario that comes to mind. I know I sleep better when I've done my planning the night before. I'm sure you will, too.

The 'Daily Dozen' Minutes

I recommend that you spend 12 minutes each day planning. 'Why 12?' I hear you say, 'it's such an odd number.' Limit yourself to 12 and you will become more disciplined about knowing how long 12 minutes actually is. In reality most of us have a very poor sense of time.

How many times have you told yourself that you're going to undertake a task for just five minutes? An hour later you're still doing it. How long are your five-minute tasks taking? Get to know what 12 minutes feels like and stick with it. I promise it'll be as natural as walking by the time you've done it for a few weeks.

In your 12 minutes, this is what you need to do:

Write All Your Tasks Down

- Open your Daily Diary at tomorrow. There may already be some items on that page that you've previously entered from your Master List. For example, if tomorrow is Wednesday the 'trousers to be taken to the dry cleaners' will appear, along with anything else you've put on that page.

- As you look at the list, think about what else you would like to achieve tomorrow and write those things down, too.

Tip! Book your holidays well in advance to ensure you get what you want and avoid stress.

What Do I Do First?

Now think about what order you need to attack your tasks.

Look at the list and decide which items are your apples. What are the urgent and valuable things that you have to complete tomorrow? Put an A next to everything that falls into this category. Then do the same with the blueberries. Decide which items are the next most important to be done, and mark them with a B. Next identify the caster sugar items, marking them with a C, and finally the wine items, marking them with a D.

Quick Reminder

A = Valuable + Urgent = Apples	Action this before anything else
B = Valuable + Non Urgent = Blueberries	Be doing this only after the 'A's are done
C = Non Valuable + Urgent = Caster sugar	Careful not to do this first or second
D = Non Valuable + Non Urgent = Wine	Don't do it until everything else is finished!

Once you've assigned every item with an A, B, C or D, return to each category and prioritize what needs to be done first. So when you look at all the As, or apples, which one needs to be tackled first? When you've decided, place a 1 by the side of that item. Put a 2 by the second, a 3 by the third and so on. When this is complete, move onto the Bs, then the Cs and the Ds.

Prioritize them in exactly the same way. One of the benefits of doing this at night is that it gives you a head-start on things you need to do. For example, with the dry-cleaning issue, seeing that you have to go to the dry cleaners the next day may well prompt you to put the trousers into the car ready for tomorrow. This has to be better than scurrying round in the morning trying to locate the trousers while making two packed lunches, buttering toast and pouring coffee all at the same time.

So, there you have it: a beautifully prioritized 'Action List' (or my Big AL as I like to call it!) ready for action in the morning – and it only took you 12 minutes. You really will sleep soundly knowing that you've done this.

Execution of the Action List

So here you are. It's the next morning, you've got a great list, it's all prioritized and you've just had your best night's sleep in ages, because you feel in control. As you look down at your list, what do you do first? No, not D7 (chat to Kathleen about where to buy cheaper pet food).

You go straight to A1 (call for prospectuses for a potential new school for Loxley), that's what you do.

The old you would have rung Kathleen immediately. Like drinking wine, this is a pleasant but unnecessary task. The new you will have the commitment and resolve to do A1 first, then A2 and then A3. D7 comes last. Do this and I promise you will feel fabulous.

Keeping Track of What You've Done

As your day progresses, keep track of your Action List using these symbols:

Completed Action – ✓

As you complete each action, tick it off. This is a delicious task. Each time we complete a task we get a little rush of endorphins. Get high on life – give yourself some ticks.

Waiting Action – W

Sometimes you start a task and you can't finish it. For example, you call someone, and they say they will get back to you with some information. You can't tick it off, but you've done everything you possibly can on this item. Just put a letter **W** by the side of it to remind yourself that it still needs to be attended to. If the person says they will get back to you next Friday, put a note to remind yourself of that commitment on next Friday's diary page.

Delegated Action – D

If you have delegated an activity to somebody – for example you've asked your husband to take back the video to Blockbuster, put a letter **D** next to the item. If he tells you he has done the task, tick it off – or, at the end of the day check with him to ensure it has been done. Once you've delegated a task you should forget about it until the time that it is due for completion. If it's required on a later day, note it on the relevant day in your diary. This will remind you to check it has been done.

Forwarded Action – F

You may have an item that for some reason you are unable to complete on a specific day. Perhaps you went to the dry cleaners and they were closed for lunch. The next chance you have to go is next Thursday. Put a letter F next to this item and move it forward to next Thursday.

Deleted Action – X

This might be something that you have decided no longer needs to be done. You decide not to go away for a long weekend in April. Now you don't have to pick up travel brochures. Cross it off your list.

Action Notes – Λ Δ

As you go through your day, things often happen that require action. A friend may ask you if she can borrow a book. Write this into the noted section of your diary. To remind yourself that you need to look at this later, draw a triangle without any bottom line next to the item. When you prepare your Daily Action List, decide what to do about the book. You might put it into your bag to hand over tomorrow, or you might make it an action for another day. Either way, close the outstanding action by drawing the bottom line onto the triangle. The third line will indicate that the action is complete.

Other Ways to Group and Prioritize Your List Logically

Things You Can't Do until Later – L

Because we live in a crazy world, sometimes it doesn't make sense to approach a list of tasks in exactly the order that they appear. For example, perhaps one of your **A** items is to exercise. It might even be your **A1** item. If you've already arranged to go running with your friend Clare in the evening, you're not going to be able to tick it off as your first item. It's certainly not my recommendation that you sit doing nothing all day until Clare appears at eight that evening! Do the sensible thing – move on to item A2, knowing that you will tick off A1 later in the day. If I have an item that I know I will do later on in the day, I often place an L next to it, to let me know that I've got permission to leave it, guilt free, until later.

Phone Calls – P

If you have a lot of calls to make, sometimes it makes sense to do them in batches. Put a **P** next to all phone calls and make them when you get a moment. That way they don't eat into core time. Differentiate between A, B, C and D calls.

E-mails – E

If you're a working mum, e-mails will quite possibly be your mainstay of communication with other human beings. As with phone calls, I mark any items on my list that are e-mails with an E. This way I can deal with them in batches.

Shopping Items – S

Anything marked with an S is a shopping item, to be dealt with when you are at the shops.

Example of a Day it All Got Done

Monday 3rd

Priority		Action	Status Notes
C2	Take trousers to dry cleaners	✔	
A4	Call Water Board re leaks	✔	Engineer will call on sixth
C4	Change car insurance	✔	
A2	20 minutes on exercise bike	✔	
C3	Buy present for Harvey and Saffy	✔	
D2	Call Lisa re when can I visit	F	Forward to next week
B1	Ten minutes' planning which schools to look at for Loxley	✔	
B5	Read 15 pages of book in a bubble bath	✔	
A3	Eat proper breakfast with kids	✔	
B3	Book baby-sitter for 25th	W	Waiting for answer

C1	Post birthday card	✔	
B2	Spend 20 minutes one-on-one, engaged, quality time with Daniel, Joshua and Jacob	✔	
A1	12 minutes' daily planning time	✔	
			Lou has asked if Jessica can buy our old guitar, dig it out of the loft △
B4	Pelvic floor exercises ten times in conjunction with another task	✔	
D1	Quick note to Susan to remind her I still exist – and ask about Luke and Alex coming to stay	F	Forward to next week

This is how you get things done in the right order. Some days it will go wrong – life has a habit of happening in ways that we don't always expect. But just imagine if the majority of the time you were managing to get the most important things done in your life. Picture the scene now: you, at the end of a day when everything is done. Everyone in your house is happy, there is a calm air. You're sipping a large glass of wine – not because you're on your knees and can't cope without a bucket of Chardonnay, but because you're having a celebratory sip of well-deserved vino. As you picture this scene, just imagine what it feels like inside. Enjoy the feeling, let your body experience it, and know that if you follow through with this, you could get used to living with a new calm and 'in control' you.

The Day it All Got Done and I Danced with Destiny

It doesn't end here, though. Imagine what it would be like if you were getting tasks that relate to your dreams and life purpose done, too. We're not talking about cleaning the sink and removing the apple cores from under Jason and Amy's bed now. We're talking about the items in your Destiny Diary.

Incorporating your higher and longer-term goals into your daily life is easy. Just do the following:

- Look at each PEP Goal in your Destiny Diary and identify the steps you'd have to take to achieve it.
- Give each of the steps a Destiny Date for completion.
- Transfer the steps into your Daily Action Lists at the appropriate time.

Destiny Planning, an Example

Here's an example. Let's say one of the goals in your Destiny Diary is to run a half-marathon. To work out the steps and Destiny Dates involved, use the following technique.

Start with your goal of running the half-marathon, then work backwards from the completion date, let's say, July, until today. Let's pretend today is 3 January.

Three Magic Questions will help you work out all the information you need:

Magic Question one: What do I need to do?
Magic Question two: When do I need to do it by?
Magic Question three: What else do I need to do?

This is how it works. First, ask Magic Question One:

Q1: What do I need to do to run a half-marathon in July?
A: I need to get fit.
Q: What do I need to do to get fit?
A: I need to train.
Q: What do I need to do to train?
A: I need to buy a book on training.
Q: What do I need to do to buy a book on training?
A: Go to a book shop.

Keep asking yourself Magic Question One, 'What do I need to do?', until you get to a tangible action, in this case going to a bookshop. Next ask Magic Question Two, 'When do I need to do it by?' **Note this as a Destiny Date.**

Q2: When do I need to go to the bookshop?
A: 5 January.

Then ask Magic Question Three:

Q3: What else do I need to do in order to run a half-marathon?
A: Read the book on training.
Q1: What do I need to do to read the book on training?
A: I need to read for 15 minutes every other day starting on 10 January.

Q2: By when do I have to complete this action?

A: 20 February. Note this as a Destiny Date.

Q3: What else do I need to do in order to run a half-marathon?

A: Find out where half-marathons are taking place...

And so it goes on, until when you ask the question, 'What else do I need to do to run a half-marathon?', the answer is 'Nothing.' You have all your action steps with destiny dates.

Half-marathon Steps	Destiny Date	Notes
Buy a book on training for marathons	5 January	Pick up when shopping in town
Start reading marathon book	10 January	15 minutes every other day (schedule in Daily Diary)
Marathon book complete	20 February	
Do any friends want to do it with me?	10 January	Spend an evening sending out e-mails to likely candidates
Find out where any marathons are taking place	15 January	Spend one evening researching on the web
Book marathon	10 February	
Work out a training schedule	30 February	

Work out childcare for when I'm training	15 February	
Train	1 March onwards	Set aside chunks of time for training
Run the half-marathon	July	

Make Your Dreams a Part of Your Destiny

- Once a week, make time to sit down with your Destiny Diary.
- If any Destiny Dates from your Diary fall in the coming week, transfer them to your Daily Diary.
- Ask yourself, 'Are there any more actions I can take this week to move me towards my desired destiny?'
- When you undertake your 'Daily Dozen' minutes of planning, prioritize these destiny actions as A, B, C or D, along with all the other tasks on that day. Then, just do them.
- Remember to have fun with your Destiny Diary. It's a living document. Amend it as your dreams change. If you're feeling creative, put drawings, images from magazines or inspirational words to motivate you further into taking action.
- As you achieve a goal or take a significant step forwards, celebrate.

You are now bringing items into your life that most people only have in their peripheral vision or blind spot. You have them in clear 20/20 perspective. How fabulous is that? And it's easy.

Who else do you know who's doing this and living the life they really want?

Actions for Week Four

- Create a prioritized Daily Action List. (12 minutes per day)
- Give the goals in your Destiny Diary some Destiny Deadlines. (Ten minutes to two hours.) Dedicate as much time to it as you can, or do it in ten-minute daily chunks – the important thing is to keep updating it, even if you only do a little at a time.
- Move actions from your Destiny Diary into your Daily Diary for the coming week. (ten minutes)
- Follow through on your plan each day.

Summary

- Failing to plan is planning to fail.
- Use the Wine Bottle Theory of Time Management to work out what's going into your jug of life.
- Prioritize your tasks based on what value they have in your life and on how urgent they are.

- Tackle your A and B tasks (apples and blueberries) first.
- Keep all your Daily Actions in your Daily Diary.
- Keep your longer-term goals in your Destiny Diary.
- Produce a prioritized Action List every evening (or first thing in the morning if this works for you).
- Use a tracking system to keep on top of what you have done.
- Incorporate the longer-term goals from your Destiny Diary into your Daily Diary on a weekly basis.

Week Five

Time Management for the Masses

An Ode to Managing the Masses

Tilly has lost her school bag again,
This chaos really sends me insane,
Susie's hockey stick, where can it be?
There's just so much stuff in here I cannot see.
Where's Ollie's lunchbox? Nobody knows,
I've lost the plot here and it really shows,
Come on Tilly, where are your shoes?
We haven't got a moment to lose.
I feel like I want to drop dead on the floor,
And we're only trying to get out the door.
Shouting and screaming I really hate,
But 'Hurry up we're going to be late,'
Why can't my family just tow the line?
So there's a slim chance we'll leave on time,
Who's doing what, with whom, when and where?
It's enough to make you tear out your hair,
We've run out of nappies, lotion and wipes,
I'll just have to improvise, use some old tights,
Divine intervention, I think we are ready,
No, Tilly has got to go back for her teddy,
All go and get in the car right now please,
I just don't believe it, now I've lost my keys.
We need a much better system in place,
So life doesn't feel like a slap in the face.

Time Truths 1 2 3 4 5 6 7

Systems save time

The Need for Super-Systems

In the early 20th century, a man called Frederick Taylor came up with a concept that changed the way we work today. He stated that by adopting a scientific approach to the way we undertake our work, we could complete tasks faster. Up until that point many people did their work in quite a haphazard way (sound familiar?). Taylor studied how people carried out the sequencing of their tasks. He timed their motions with the ultimate aim of determining the most efficient way to perform a particular job. His work marked the beginnings of what we now know as time-and-motion studies.

His theory was that even the most basic, mindless and boring tasks could be planned in such a way that they could be completed faster. As most of us undertake a plethora of mindless and boring tasks during a typical day, it struck me that this is a theory we could perhaps use to decrease the amount of time we spend on them. Plenty of other people have used it to good effect in the past, so why not mums?

Managing the Masses

In 1913, Henry Ford revolutionized the automotive industry with the introduction of the production line. For the first time, cars were produced en masse, for the masses. This was made possible by the use of streamlined procedures. Instead of components being brought to the car, the car was moved along an assembly line and taken to the components. This revolution in systems engineering meant that more cars could be made faster than ever before.

Back in the 1950s, the Japanese honed production processes even further. They stole the world stage from America and Europe in car manufacture, using a technique known as 'Just-in-Time Management'. Components were ordered and brought to the production line just as they were needed. There was no slack in the system and no cost of waiting stock. Profits soared.

The Mass Production of Family Life

When you had children, suddenly you got into mass production. Mass production of meals, mass organization of people and, possibly, occasional thoughts of mass murder as you struggled to figure out how to keep this multiple mass of mess and mayhem under control. We poor mums not only have to manage ourselves – now how easy would that be? – we have to manage a load of other people, too. The lesson we can draw from industry is that mass production requires great systems. Great systems save time, and very often money.

Systemizing those things that we know are going to happen from day to day gives us the freedom to forget about them, safe in the knowledge that they will happen at a set time, just when they need to. More importantly, it frees up our brain space, removing the need to carry everything around in our heads on mental Post-it notes. We set up a system or a process and then let it run itself. We're then free as birds to be creative and spontaneous in other areas of our lives. There's a lot we can learn from the world of business and manufacturing about how to maximize our productivity.

Systematic or Problematic, Which One Is Your Life?

Take a look at these questions. What do they tell you about how systematic you are?

Something to think about ...	*Agree*	*Disagree*	*Partly agree*
I have no idea where all my time goes.	❑	❑	❑
You often think that you've been reincarnated as a parrot, due to the number of times you repeatedly ask members of your family to do simple jobs that would save you time.	❑	❑	❑
You are constantly doing things that you think should be somebody else's responsibility (flushing the toilet after lazy eight-year-olds, for example).	❑	❑	❑
You seem to spend an inordinate amount of your spare time cooking and cleaning up.	❑	❑	❑
Apart from things you have to do like pre-school, school and work, there's no real routine in your life, things just happen when they happen.	❑	❑	❑
You have a migraine for a week just thinking about what you have to pack to go on a family holiday.	❑	❑	❑
You find getting out of the house en masse, and on time, nigh-on impossible. You are always shouting frantically to your children, 'Will you hurry up and get ready?!'	❑	❑	❑

You have no foolproof system for dealing with all the paper and information that comes into your house. Things often get misplaced, and people often can't find what they are looking for.	❑	❑	❑
If you just had to manage yourself you'd be fine, but coping with the family you find somewhat chaotic.	❑	❑	❑
You're always hunting for things and getting things ready for other people at the last minute.	❑	❑	❑
Nobody else in your house seems to know where anything goes.	❑	❑	❑

Tip! *Get school holidays and event dates into your diary well in advance.*

The Rules and Tools of Winning Systems

If you agreed with a number of these statements, then your lack of systematic organization is probably costing you time, energy and money. You need systems. So, here it is, the Manic Mum's Guide to Systems that Save Time. This chapter gives you the top-ten rules and tools for taking a systematic approach to your life and work. A good system, process or routine will save you time. It increases your productivity by decreasing the gap between the time a task could take and the time that it actually does take. Some of the systems are straightforward and can be implemented immediately. Others will require an up-front investment of time.

Although these are systems that apply to your home, some of them will work just as well in an office setting. For ExecuMums who want a tranquil and organized work life too, try them out in both environments.

In your Daily Dozen planning minutes, setting up a new system will show up as an important but non-urgent task. It's a blueberry. As we now know, these are the activities that will produce the watch cogs of your life. The opportunity cost of not doing them will be your loss of time. Come on, work smarter, not harder, and take a lot less time to get everything done. Have more time for little old you to do more of what you want.

Rule One – Know What's Going on at All Times

Tool One – The 'PPP': People and Place Planner

The first tool to help you systemize is to find a way of capturing what everybody is up to in your house. To schedule the masses, invest in a large wall planner that can be placed where every member of your family can see it. This way, everybody knows what everybody else is supposed to be doing. Include your husband in this. Past experience tells me that most married men feel like the blind being led by the partially sighted when it comes to pinpointing what their family and they themselves are supposed to be up to. Put them on the planner – blissful ignorance is no longer an excuse.

A wall planner may seem like a rudimentary device, and I have to say I envisage a day when we'll have fruit in the fruit bowl, milk in the fridge and huge computer screens stuck on the larder door. Whether your kitchen looks like the Star Ship Enterprise or you use a paper wall planner, it's the principle and mindset of doing this that are most important rather than the tool you use to capture it all. If you can use Outlook Express, or some other team-planning tool, all the better. Whatever works for you. The system needs to accommodate a space each day for every member of your family. If you have a nanny or an au pair, give them a space, too. They are critical cogs in the organizational machinery of your home.

Put all the activities that happen on a regular basis onto the planner: swimming lessons, ballet lessons, music lessons, that sort of thing. Then as other activities come in, post them onto the calendar, too. Ideally you'll have a note of all this in your Daily Diary as well. Being able to see at a glance what is going on gives you an instant sense of control. If you're a working mum, block out your work hours on the planner so everyone knows when you are available. This is particularly important for mums who work from home. Make sure everyone can see when you are working. This will assist in keeping boundaries between work and home time clear.

Tip! *Get small children to join in with chores. They love helping. Although your four-year-old's dusting might not be quite up to your standard, they will see it as play and it's a great way to spend quality time with them.*

From the Mouths of Mums:

'My daughter had been invited to a birthday party, which I had forgotten all about. I'd written it in my work diary, but not my home diary. A crazy thing to do, really. I received a phone call at 10.30 asking where my daughter was. My daughter was still in her pyjamas, as was I! I quickly pulled on her party frock and bundled her into the car. I looked like I'd just been dragged through a hedge backwards, and was really embarrassed that I hadn't even been able to remember such a simple thing as arriving at a party. I had no gift, and a very cross daughter.'

Rule Two – No Mess

I don't know about you, but for a number of years my house looked like it had exploded. On every surface in every room there was stuff. Leaflets, banana skins, toys, letters from school, shopping lists, last year's telephone directory, the Chinese takeaway menu, the appointment letter for my husband's vasectomy, and so many other things I couldn't tell you.

They'd been buried for so long I'd forgotten what they were. I might even have had a fourth child, lost under a pile somewhere! How many times had I found myself searching for crucial pieces of paper that I knew couldn't be far away? Some of the clutter mountains were so high I needed a harness and full climbing gear to get to the peak.

How much time did I waste looking for missing pieces of jigsaw, lost teddies and Toy Boys (whoops, I mean Game Boys)? Why was it when I needed something I could never find it? Why was it when the children needed something, they couldn't find it either? I had no foolproof system for ensuring the house was kept tidy. In true Manic Martha style I was always chasing around clearing up after everyone else. I often said to the children I felt like I was running a hotel, because I did everything. The problem was that, unlike your average hotel, which runs like clockwork thanks to extensive systems and procedures, our house was more like Fawlty Towers. On a Wednesday, when she was feeling brave enough, the cleaner came in. She took two steps forward and three steps back in her efforts to spruce up my house. It was hopeless. We had to get organized, but where on earth do you start? How about the room that would make the most difference to your life if you get it sorted?

Tool Two – The Bite-sized Room Blitz

- Make a concerted effort to clear up one room at a time.
- Set a time frame to complete the whole room.
- Chunk the job down into manageable tasks – one drawer or cupboard a day, for example. Include these tasks in your Daily Action List. They'll probably show up as B tasks – of value but not that urgent. The important thing is to make a start and keep going. Bit by bit until it's done.
- In severe cases, call in the clutter-clearing police and get a professional to make it happen.

The Ten-minute Tidy

Once a room is basically tidy it's relatively easy to keep it that way, with a small amount of effort. Just bring it into your near focus for ten minutes, then banish it to your peripheral vision until the next tidy. Here's how:

- Have all your dusters and cleaning products in one basket that you can pick up and carry round.
- Collect up the items strewn in the room. Put the ones that belong in the room in one basket, put the rest in another basket.
- With the debris gone, give a quick flick round with the duster.
- Straighten pillows, tidy magazines and ornaments.
- Sweep or vacuum the floor.
- If you're done with minutes to spare, put away the items in the two baskets, or give it to someone else to do. Then sit down in your lovely clean room and relax.

The Ten-minute Bombsite Blitz (Your Kid's Bedroom)

- Work with your children to get their room up to scratch by doing a big room blitz.
- Let your children know that ten minutes a day will be dedicated to tidying their room.
- Collect all washing and put it in the washing basket.

- Make the bed.
- Collect everything that is lying around and put it in a basket.
- Put away clean clothes.
- Put away the things from the basket.
- Weekly vacuum and dust.
- Prepare a checklist, so if your children are old enough they can do these jobs for themselves each day. Try to make it fun. For example, do it to music. Say you'll tidy for the duration of three songs. Play around and engage your children. I've found that there is something about sticking your tongue in and out in time to the music as you tidy that makes small children laugh in a way I'll never quite understand. (Warning, this absolutely does not work with teenagers!)

Keeping Things Clear For Ever

According to Clare Draper, founder of the Clutter Clearing Consultancy, it's possible to keep on top of your clutter in only ten minutes a day. Here's what she says:

'We at CCC teach people to create a new clutter-clearing and control "habit". People who keep on top of their clutter and mess are those who have turned the process into a habit, by investing the time to do it 20 times. They soon find that they don't have to think consciously about it and can easily and quickly tidy up within about ten minutes a day.'

Give it 20 days and that could be you.

Rule Three – Don't Put it Down, Put it Away

Tool Three – Possessions with a Place to Go

As a Mum coach, one of the biggest complaints I hear about offspring is how messy they are and how they never put anything away, leaving Mum to sort everything out.

From the Mouths of Mums:

'Every day without fail I pick up coats, shoes and school bags from where they have been dumped at the back door. I'm fed up of spending all my time nagging and clearing up, I feel like a slave.'

On average, mums spend about four hours a week cleaning and picking up. If you do, does it get on your nerves? Is the bane of your life clearing up other people's mess? If not, you're quite possibly the only mother in existence who doesn't mind. Prevention, of course, is always better than cure. If your children are young, get them into the routine of putting things away. Each time they finish playing with something, ask them to put it back. Get them used to the idea of spending a small amount of time in the middle of the day, and at the end of the day, clearing away.

I know one mum whose daughter is partially sighted. Their house is always completely tidy; it has to be. If you can't see very well, you need to know that things are exactly where you expect them to be. Everything has a place so items can always be found. From a very early age she has learned to put things back when she finished with them. Most of us don't instil these habits into our children and then wonder why they leave us with loads to clear up. The motto is, start young. This way you are building good habits, and an expectation in your children that they do have some responsibility to keep the house tidy.

For the 'Don't put it down, put it away' rule to work, everything must have a place to go. Shoes must have a shelf, coats must have a peg, and school bags must have a resting place. Everybody needs to know where these places are. Scissors, sticky tape, glue, stamps, string – all must have a home of their own. When they've been used they must be put back from whence they came. Think about the things you most often have to clear up, or search for. Assign them a home. Make sure everyone else knows where the home is. Here are a few suggestions for the types of items you can group together in a box and keep in one place:

Needlework kit
Medical kit
Children's medicine box
Children's craft box
Puncture-repair kit
Battery box
Lightbulb box
Shoe-cleaning box
Hair-tie and brush box
Wrapping-up box

Note pad for phone messages with pen attached
Homework kit (pens, pencils, ruler, calculator etc).

From the Mouths of Mums:

'I got so fed up of never being able to find goggles on swimming day and tutus on ballet day, I bought an activity bag for each child. I put all the relevant kit for each activity in the labelled bag and hung it by the door. When Leila goes to ballet, I put the ballet clothes straight back into the bag after the lesson. No more running round the house like a headless chicken, raising a search party for a ballet shoe every Thursday.'

The more rigour you can get around these types of systems, the easier your life will be.

Tip! *Make a list of the people you want to send birthday cards to in month order. At the start of each month, write out all the cards for that month and put a posting date on the envelope.*

Rule Four – Put it Down, it Will Be Purged

Tool Four – The One-warning Pile-purger

If people disobey Rule Three, here's another way to deal with their time-stealing mess. It might seem harsh, but you don't have time to be constantly tidying up. Cull carnage from your kitchen, banish it from your bathroom and purge it from the play room. Become a pile-purger.

- Decide what items you are not prepared to have lying around. For example, toys that haven't been put away, pyjamas that have not been put under the pillow, washing that hasn't been put in the basket, etc.
- Make it clear to everybody in your family that from next week you will be following a system to eliminate messy piles, and it doesn't involve the use of Anusol cream. This system involves the use of a basket.
- Purchase a basket. You may want to have one for each room, depending on how prolific your piles are.
- On a daily basis, collect anything that has been left in a pile and place it in the basket.
- At the end of each week, or on a specified day, for example, a Friday, make it clear that you will empty the basket and dispose of the items in it.
- Specify what warning you will give before disposing of anything. Be consistent in your actions.
- Your family will soon realize that you mean business, thus removing the need for nagging. (Nagging, by the way, is a complete waste of

time. It's as useful as a wet cardboard box when it comes to galvanizing others into action.)

- Stick to the system. As long as everybody understands the rules, this system works brilliantly. It is crucial that you get agreement from everybody before you start and that everybody understands and agrees to the consequences of not putting things away.

Rule Five – Everyone Must Pull their Weight

'Ask not what you can do for other people, but what other people can do for you.'

In the 1980s a great business commentator called Charles Handy developed the concept of the Clover Leaf Organisation.

He recognized that high-performing companies stuck to their core business and outsourced everything else. For example, a car manufacturer would manufacture cars. It wouldn't clean the factory and it wouldn't run the canteen. These things didn't form part of its core business. It passed these jobs to other organizations, leaving it free to bring into near focus what was valuable and important to it: the manufacture of cars.

The concept of outsourcing to gain leverage is one we can use in the family. What would it be like if you were somehow able to outsource the tasks that didn't add value to your life, the ones that weren't what you really wanted to focus on? Think back to your Eye of

Time. What did you want to move to your peripheral vision or blind spot?

Often people say they feel guilty if they're not doing everything themselves, but being a martyr doesn't get you more time. Come on, have a think. Who and what can you outsource? Before you cry, 'I can't afford to outsource my jobs,' let me assure you this doesn't have to entail paying someone else. Partnering up with a neighbour or friend to do a babysitting swap will get you leverage. You pay for it by providing childcare in return; it costs you nothing. If you had an au pair who could do many jobs for you, how many hours would you have to work to pay for it? You might only have to work for eight hours to pay for her 30, a great swap. What could you do with 30 hours of help?

Tool Five – Outrageous Outsourcing

Use this tool on employees, children, husbands and friends. See what you can delegate today. Think of a task to outsource and follow the guidelines below.

- Agree with the person you are outsourcing to, what has to be done, when it has to be done and how it has to be done. Make sure you get a verbal agreement, particularly from children.
- Ensure they know exactly what has to be done. Check if they need any support. For example, the bins must be put out every Monday night next to the gate. On a Monday you will support them by reminding them – only once! – that it is Monday.

- Leave them to get on with it. Don't nag them 20 times on Monday night to do the job, or rush to do the job yourself. Leave them to do it, that's what delegation is all about.
- At the last minute, check that the job has been done.
- Let natural consequences come into play if they don't do the job, e.g. loss of pocket money, treats, TV, etc.

From the Mouths of Mums:

'Recently I was able to delegate the house cleaning to my teenage daughter. She was delighted because she got more pocket money for doing it. I was delighted because it saved me from doing the curse that is cleaning. I had to spend a bit of time up front getting very clear about what I wanted, because to start off with her idea of cleaning and mine were quite different.'

Exercise – Delicious Delegation

- Make a list of all the jobs that you have to do now.
- Think of all the possible resources you have available to outsource them to.

- Decide what you will outsource.
- Try to think of something that can be outsourced on a regular basis so you can build it into your routine.
- Make it happen.

From the Mouths of Mums:

'Last year I outsourced Christmas dinner to my 11 house guests. I decided to give each person a job to do towards the lunch – the turkey, the pudding, the cheese and biscuits. Even the children had a job. I'm used to doing it all myself, so this was a bit of a stretch for me. All I did was the vegetables. Do you know what? I had a lovely day and I wasn't exhausted and everyone felt like they'd contributed to the success of the day.'

Here are a few ideas to help you outrageously outsource.

Potential Resources	Jobs to Outsource
Children	Three- to four-year-olds put toys away, help fold washing, pair socks, put their own rubbish in the bin, put washing in the basket, water plants, help with dusting, feed pets

	Five- to six-year-olds: wipe the bathroom sink, put cutlery away, set the table, sort washing into colour piles, take dishes to the sink Seven- to nine-year-olds: take out the rubbish, clear the table, vacuum and clean their room, empty the dishwasher, put away dishes, water the garden Nine- to eleven-year-olds: make their own packed lunch, clean kitchen surfaces and sink, put away shopping, load the dishwasher, put away own laundry, run small errands 13–14-year-olds: clean the bathroom, change bed sheets, mow the lawn, wash the car, do washing and ironing 15 years and up: clean the fridge, make dinner – most of the things you could do with the exception of running a taxi service
Friends	Childcare, lift-shares, jobs they can do but you can't. What can you swap with them that's easy for you to do, but gets some time in return?
Parents	Mums and dads are just great for so many things, I don't know where to begin
Extended family	Childcare, odd jobs
Godparents	Childcare
Nanny	Child-related jobs, keeping rooms tidy, playroom tidy, clearing car of children's mess, cooking meals and freezing them for you to use at the weekend. Children's laundry and homework

Au pair	Babysitting, cleaning, cooking and childcare, shopping, dog-walking, administration and ironing
Gardener	Everything garden related
Childminder	If you have small children and just need a couple of hours to yourself, book a session once a week, buy yourself time
Pre-school	A couple of hours' reprieve!
Cleaner	Cleaning
Ironing service	Ironing
Cooking services	Here I include ready-made meals, the local takeaway. Even if you outsource one meal a week, how great would that be? Quite often a trip to the takeaway is a result of having nothing in the fridge or a lack of will and energy to cook. How would it be if you knew that every second Friday was takeaway night?
Virtual PA services	Use them like a personal PA; for an hourly rate they will organize your life for you. There are loads on the internet
Concierge services	Holiday-booking, taxi-booking and restaurant reservations. Many banks now run concierge services. Is this something you can get as part of your bank account?
Hot offices	Phone-answering, admin
Accountants	Tax returns, financial planning

Handyman	General house maintenance
School	Consider after-school clubs and activities to buy you more time. Your children could be doing something they love
Holiday camps	Get a bit of respite during the holidays
Valet	Car cleaning inside and out
Clothes shopping	Book an appointment with a personal shopper each season to save time picking what to wear. Many High Street stores now have them and they cost nothing. Well, apart from the clothes you end up buying
Food shopping	Harness the power of the internet and get it delivered to your door. Develop a rolling menu as shown in Rule Six
Husband	Took a while to think of one, but got it: teach him how to cook one meal and let him make it every second Saturday. (Bread and cheese won't hurt you twice a month!)

Tip! Buy a job-lot of greetings cards, thank you cards, blank cards and children's birthday cards. Keep them all in one place so they're handy when you need one. Keep a stock of stamps nearby, and also in your purse.

Now, I realize that you would probably have to take out a second mortgage to outsource everything. I've often fancied the idea of my own personal maid and chauffeur. It's not going to happen. However, let this give you a bit of inspiration. Are there things you could be delegating that you're not? When you look at the list does it inspire you to think of a cost-effective option? Let me give you a great example from a client of mine.

Cookie Nookie Night

This particular mum had been working all hours, as had her husband. Her children and spouse had become quite neglected. They were like ships that passed in the night. Romance wasn't high on the agenda either. Both of them were always working and very tired. This mum, let's call her Julia, recognized that this wasn't healthy and wanted romance back in her near focus, before it became a problem. She couldn't afford a babysitter or expensive meals out, but wanted to do something.

The solution? Cookie Nookie Night!

Julia focused on producing a romantic meal at home. To make it easy on herself she outsourced the catering to a local supermarket. She used a microwave ready meal. She dressed it up with a ready-made salad, laid a romantic, candle-lit table and dimmed the lights. The whole exercise took about ten minutes and involved very little effort.

When her husband came home they had a fabulous feast with a chilled bottle of wine. It really was a great success. Cookie Nookie Night is now a regular feature in this household. Julia and her husband take it in turns to 'cook' on a Friday. With the kids in bed, one gets things ready and the other has a glass of wine while relaxing in the bath. Try it out for yourself. I promise this is outsourcing that won't cost the earth.

Don't waste time adding spice to your cooking, add it to your life instead.

From the Mouths of Mums:

'I recently joined a babysitting circle. It's made a real difference to my social life and it's free babysitting. To be honest I even quite like just going to someone else's house for a change. The kids are usually asleep and I have a really relaxing evening watching the telly or reading a book.'

Rule Six – Routine Rules the Roost

Tool Six – Recognizing Routines

We all have our little habits and routines. Some of them save us time, some of them don't. We don't want to turn ourselves into robots, but a lack of routine can slow down family life considerably. Some of us love routine – the Perfect Paulas of the world, for example. Others feel tied by routine and structure, but without it, managing the masses becomes untenable.

Many times I speak to frazzled mums whose time-management problems stem from lack of routine. I once spoke to someone who would spend up to 45 minutes every night trying to persuade her son to read. This was a routine, but not a time-saving one.

Routines or systems around things like homework, bed and meals can save loads of time. The trick is ensuring everyone knows the routine and sticks to it.

Get more structure around your own personal routines, the ones that you have total control over. Something that always seems to help people save time is an evaluation of their morning routine. How long does it take you to get up and get yourself ready? If you thought about it, how much time could you shave off each morning by systematizing what you do?

From the Mouths of Mums:

'It never occurred to me that I could perhaps save a bit more time in the morning. Just little things, but it saved a few minutes here and there. I had my make-up done in a department store and bought what they recommended. I used the products to create the same look every day. It only took me a few minutes.
Quite often I'd go out with no make-up on because I thought it didn't really matter. I feel much better about myself now because I always look OK. Previously I decided each day what I would wear, and it took me much longer. Now I put my clothes and the children's clothes out the night before. We all look slightly more put together. I've shown them how to get dressed themselves. While they do that I make breakfast. When they come down, we actually have time to eat together. Before I would make breakfast and eat at the same time. The whole routine is much less stressful than before.'

Examples of routines you could systemize are:

- Getting up
- Getting dressed
- Bathtime
- Bedtime
- Homework
- Mealtimes
- Music practice
- Tidying up
- Setting the table
- Preparing school bags
- Preparing school uniform for the next day
- Chores
- Washing
- Ironing
- Cleaning
- Personal grooming.

Tip! Been asked to make cakes for the school fête? Buy some from a supermarket, put them on a paper plate, sprinkle them with icing sugar and, hey presto!

From the Mouths of Mums:

'Since my third baby's arrival I've delegated running the bath to Jack (seven). Fetching

pyjamas and placing laundry in the basket have been given as a job to Ellis (five). This saves me time every night. I can concentrate on the baby. My kids love the responsibility. They don't even have to be reminded.'

Start children with routines as young as possible. They need and like the structure and boundaries routines provide. Ensure that anybody who has a part in the running of your house knows what your routines are. I'm thinking particularly of nannies, grannies or anyone who is looking after your children.

Consistency is important if routines are to be upheld. For some help on getting your family into a routine, see the section on getting the family to join in (page 203).

From the Mouths of Mums:

'I used to do the washing when the basket became so full we couldn't put another pair of smelly socks in it. Now I've got into the habit of taking one load of washing down with me every day, before breakfast. I put it in the tumble dryer when I get in from work. I fold it and put it away when I go up to bed. Because there's never very much, this routine is quick. I never have loads of clothes lying around waiting to be ironed any more. I've taught my two older children how to put their own laundry away.'

Tip! *Pay all bills by standing order or direct debit.*

Exercise

Identify all the routines you have at the moment. Think about how you could streamline them further, or make them more systematic. Identify areas where more of a routine would be helpful to you.

The Mother of All Routines

How much time do you waste thinking about what to cook? How much time do you spend cooking and then clearing up after your children have refused to eat what you've prepared? For mums, the biggest percentage of their time after sleep and work is spent on food preparation.

On average, working mums spend about nine hours a week on food preparation and serving. For stay-at-home mums it's 17. It's like we're on a never-ending conveyer belt. With a good system, though, there's lots of things we can do to make our lives easier in the kitchen.

Mealtimes, the Recipe for Success

Does a top chef turn up at the restaurant each day and wonder, 'What are we going to cook today?' Of course not, and neither should we. Take a leaf out of a restaurateur's book and develop a rolling menu. One that spans two weeks is great and takes the stress and angst out of cooking. The witching hour that is teatime can be one of the most stressful and frenzied parts of a mum's day. With a meal plan you can cook ahead, bulk-cook and freeze meals. Never again will you find yourself with your head in the freezer, wondering what on earth to toss in the microwave.

A meal plan allows you to schedule healthy meals rather than last-minute pizza or chicken nuggets. This also makes shopping a dream. Developing an internet shopping list that allows you to order quickly all the required ingredients for the week ahead is easy. Mums spend around two and a half hours a week shopping. Developing this type of system is a sure-fire way to reduce this figure. Give it a try; you'll surprise yourself.

Become the Queen of Quick Cuisine

Developing your own two-week rolling menu is easy:

- Write a list of all the foods and meals your children like.
- Ask your children for ideas, too. Involve them in the process, then they're more likely to eat what you cook.
- Make a note of the meals you've eaten over the past week.
- Get hold of a couple of recipe books to inspire you.
- Split a large piece of paper into 14 columns and begin to plan out meals for lunch and dinner for two weeks.

- For each meal, write out the key ingredients onto a shopping list.
- As you do this, think about what days you have activities on. Would a slow-cooker meal work better on Thursdays and sandwiches, soup and salad on Fridays? Make the menu fit around your lifestyle.
- Get agreement from everyone and stick the menu up on the wall.

I tend to choose nutritious dishes that can be made in bulk and frozen so they only require heating up when they next appear on my menu. I've found that doing this is as quick as chicken nuggets or other 'cardboard' food. Just take very basic recipes, make them as simple as possible, and try to make them even healthier by throwing in a few seeds, garlic, some bran and serving them with boiled frozen vegetables. Since becoming a mum I've become the queen of quick cuisine. These are the kind of five-minute meals I dish up:

- Spaghetti bolognese
- Fish pie
- Chicken casserole with couscous
- Vegetarian chilli con carne
- Bacon-and-pesto pasta
- Tuna pasta
- Home-made pizza (with a breadmaker this is really quick, honest)
- Slow-cook casserole

From the Mouths of Mums:

'I adopted the approach of outsourcing rolling menus to my daughter's sandwich box. She's ten.The deal was, if she wanted to have a packed lunch she would have to make it herself. We developed a rolling midday menu.

'I make sure she has the ingredients she needs to make her lunch. It all gets ordered on the internet shop.'

Tip! *Put a sock on your hand. As you walk round the house use it to dust things. You might look a bit weird, but hey, you're a mum and it goes with the territory!*

Rolling Routines

Think of all the things in your house that never get done because there is no routine to them. I'm thinking about cleaning the carpets, getting the car washed. These are things that happen on a more infrequent basis, but you want to keep on top of them.

Make a list of everything you want to do, even if it's only once a year or once every two years. How frequently does this action need to be taken: weekly, monthly, annually, every three years?

When you've got this, schedule each item into your diary for the next year. Items that appear further away than a year, put into your Destiny Diary. Make a diary note to review this list and update it once a year. You'll have loads of your own, but here are some examples:

Action	Frequency	When will it happen?	Where do I record it?
Update annual schedule	Annually	10 January	Diary
Dental check	6-monthly	May and November	Diary
Eye test	6-monthly	February and August	Diary
General health check	Annually	September	Diary
Facial for me	6-weekly	Every 6th Saturday	Diary
Car valet	6-weekly	Every 6th Saturday	Diary
House carpets shampooed	Annually	January	Diary
Check house for maintenance jobs and book handyman	6-monthly	July, January	Diary
Central-heating and appliance safety checks	Annually	September	Diary
Check smoke alarms	3-monthly	15th of Jan, April, July, Oct	Diary
Windows cleaned	6-weekly	Tell window cleaner to come every 6 weeks	
Gutters cleared	6-monthly	February and August	Diary
Take work team out for lunch	2-monthly	Every 8th week	Diary
Clear paper work from office	6-monthly	March and September	Diary
Smear tests	3 years		Destiny Diary

Exercise

Create a rolling schedule. Put it in your Destiny Diary. Keep adding to it as you think of more things. It's a living dynamic document.

Rule Seven – Handle Paper and Information Only Once

Tool Seven – Dealing with Information Overload

How much time do you waste on average looking for letters or information that, with a good system, you'd be able to put your hands on immediately? Apparently executives spend up to 60 minutes a week looking for pieces of paper. That's 52 hours a year – what a waste! You could be on a romantic mini-break for the weekend with that kind of time on your hands!

To get yourself on top of your Paper Mountains, you need to become businesslike in your approach to the challenge. The business of organizing family paperwork isn't complicated stuff. You just need to understand a few simple tools and rules. The first thing is to gather the equipment you'll need:

- One in-tray each for Mum and Dad
- A plastic envelope for each child over the age of five
- A concertina file with 31 tabs (monthly)
- A concertina file with 12 tabs (annual)

Mapping the Paper Trail

With your tools in hand, you're ready to map out the new journey that will be taken by paper or information as it enters your house. When a piece of paper comes your way, don't just toss it to one side to be dealt with later. Ask yourself the following questions:

- Can I do it?
- Can I dump it?
- Can I delegate it?
- Does it go in the in-tray?

Your mantra for all paper will be: DO it, DUMP it, DELEGATE or TRAY it.

Can I Do It?

Look at your paper and ask yourself, 'Can I do it?' If the answer to this question is 'Yes', then just do it. As a rule of thumb, if the action required takes less than a few minutes, do it there and then. When Jessica comes home with a letter from school requesting payment for the school trip, deal with it right there and then. Write out the cheque, note any dates and actions you need to take in your Daily Diary and put the cheque and letter straight back in her school bag, to return the following day, job done.

Tip! *Put the pen by the phone on a string so it doesn't disappear.*

Can I Dump It?

Be ruthless as paper comes into your house and seriously ask this question. Do I need this or could I just throw it away? Does someone else have it, or is it easy to retrieve if I really do need it? Take great joy in tossing it in the recycling or wastepaper basket.

Can I Delegate It?

I can't tell you what a joyous feeling I get when I open a piece of post and realize that it's something my husband has to deal with. I know I'm sad, but I jump for joy as I toss the paper over the top of my in-tray and watch it land in his. Putting it in someone else's in-tray prevents you from being distracted by it. You've got quite enough to do without having to deal with the paperwork of others, thank you very much.

Does It Go in the In-tray?

If you can't do it, dump it or delegate it, you will still have the paper in your hand. Resist the overriding temptation to pop it onto the nearest available worktop as you promise yourself you'll deal with it later. No, just place it into your trusty in-tray.

You must have one definitive place to put all items of information that require processing. Please, stop using your refrigerator, or worse still your house, as a giant paper receptacle. I can't tell you the number of times I've had to pull off a year's worth of old literature from the fridge. Use your fridge as an ice tray, not an in-tray.

Have one in-tray each for Mum and Dad, and a plastic envelope for each child. Store them next to your in-tray. Any member of the family who is bringing information into or out of your house on a regular basis needs an in-tray or an envelope. Once safely placed in your in-tray, paper will patiently wait to be processed later. When I say 'later' I don't mean next week or – judging by the state of some people's houses – next year. You need to process it that same day.

Tip! *Get your children to set the table and clear up their own plates.*

Empty the In-tray

You may have noticed that the average in-tray is about 15cm deep. This is similar in depth to the average tea tray, as opposed to the depth and width of the average skip. There is a reason for this. You're supposed to empty it diligently every day. 'No,' I hear you scream in terror as you imagine your tall pile of parchment torturously toppling on you as you try to wade through it at one sitting. The motto here is 'little and often'.

Get your system up and running and it will be as easy as clockwork. The reason most people's in-trays become hideously full is that they don't know what to do with the paper that's in them. More often than not they look at it gingerly as they shuffle it around on the table. This gives the impression that they are actually doing something with it. After wasting ten minutes doing nothing, they put it back in the in-tray before putting more stuff on top of it. Your in-tray is a holding area, not permanent storage.

Here is the definitive guide to getting on top of your in-tray.

- Take the first piece of paper and work down the pile.
- Remember, the object is to handle each piece of paper only once. From the in-tray, paper goes directly to its final destination. If you want to know how much time you waste messing about with papers, put a red dot on each piece of admin every time you touch it. If your papers start to look like they've contracted a contagious disease, it's time for a sea change.
- For each piece of paper ask yourself :
    1. What actions do I need to take now?
    2. What actions do I need to take later?
    3. Where does this piece of paper need to be stored?

An Example of Perfect Paper Handling

Imagine that the item you have just opened is an invitation to a party on the 23rd of next month. Let's think about how you might tackle this so everything happens when it should.

What Actions Do I Need to Take Now?

- *Check your calendar. Can you go?*

  With your Daily Diary next to you, this is a relatively easy task. If the answer is 'Yes', write it in straight away.

- *Tell your other half to put it in his diary.*

  Write a quick e-mail or a note and put it in his in-tray, so he can process it later.

- *Reply to the invite.*

  You can do this straightaway, maybe by e-mail (don't be distracted by other e-mails). Or drop a short acceptance note. Your in-tray area should have, nearby, a stock of pens, cards, paper envelopes and stamps to ensure that you can complete this type of task without having to run all over your house looking for a reply card and a Biro that works.

- *Book a babysitter.*

  This is a phone call or text. If you get an answer straightaway, that part of the job is complete. If not, leave a message. This action is pending completion. Put the action of chasing the sitter into your Daily Diary Action List for Tuesday. If by then you've not heard back, you'll remember to call again. This task will appear magically on the day you want it to.

What Actions Do I Need to Take Later?

- *Buy a gift that looks like some thought went into it.*

  If you're sitting by your in-tray, chances are you won't be buying the gift right now, unless of course you want to do a bit of internet shopping. If not, schedule gift-buying into your Daily Diary. When you've purchased the gift, wrap it immediately and put it in an obvious place to be remembered. In our house we have a box in the cellar where we keep wrapping paper and any gifts we have bought in advance, so we all know where they are.

- *Get some new shoes to go with your outfit.*

  Those all-essential shoes. Perhaps plan to get them at the same time as the gift. Put the action into your Diary for the day you plan to buy them.

Where Does this Piece of Paper Need to be Stored?

Where do you put the invite so you can lay your hands on it exactly when you need it? The answer is to use bring-forward and filing systems like the ones described below. These will ensure that you can always find whatever you need, whenever you want.

The Miracle of Storage and Filing Systems

Retrieving things just when you need them can sometimes be a challenge. Effective storage and filing systems will help solve this problem. We'll talk about filing systems later, but first let me introduce you to the daily and monthly bring-forward file.

You should have in your possession two concertina bring-forward files, one monthly, with 31 tabs, and one annual, with 12 tabs. If you have an item that you want to reappear at a particular date, at any time in the next month, pop it in the monthly file, in the pocket number that corresponds with the date you want it to appear. In our case, pocket number 23, the day of the party. I guarantee that it will jump out just when you need it. How? As part of your Daily Dozen planning routine, take all the papers from your bring-forward file for the day you are about to plan and put them into your in-tray for processing. So, on the evening of the 22nd you would take out all the papers from pocket number 23 and put them in your empty in-tray. Hey presto! The invite and directions appear just when you want them, on the 23rd.

The 31-day bring-forward file is a fabulous folder for storing anything that you want to deal with at some point in the next month. For example, you might get a bill on 3 November due to be paid on the 27th. You could take action now. Write and post-date the check. Put it in a stamped, addressed envelope and place it in the bring-forward file on the day that you want to post it, say the 25th. It will reappear on the 25th. Alternatively, you could put the bill to come into your focus on the day you want to deal with it. This will be some time before the 27th; let's say the 24th. It will appear on the 24th.

Provided you go through your file every day, using this system you can quickly file things confident that they will reappear when you want them.

The 12-month bring-forward file works in exactly the same way as the monthly one. Use this for things you'll need in the next 12 months. You might be given a catalogue that looks like it has some good potential Christmas gifts. Thing is, it's only January. So file it in the August pocket of your system and it will pop out then when you want to see it.

I often ask my clients to write themselves a letter about what they want to achieve in the next year. I then send it to them a year later. The way I remember to send it in exactly 12 months' time is to place it in my 12-month bring-forward file.

Then, in the relevant month the following year, I put it into my 31-day bring-forward file. I post it to them on exactly the day they were expecting it, one year after they wrote it. I don't have to give it a second thought from one year to the next, because I know my system ensures things happen when they should.

Effective Filing Systems

All other paper that doesn't need to go into a bring-forward file must be put into hanging files or ring-binder files. Each file needs a title that relates directly to what is in it. Use sticky labels or invest in a labelling machine. Call me sad, but I love mine, it makes my files look so much more businesslike.

Having smart files just makes me feel more organized and in control. The files should be stored alphabetically. Titles might include Bills, Ideas, Garden, Building Work, School Letters, Bank Statements, Directions, Dream Holidays, Work, Destiny Diary, etc.

If you've not got much shelf space, use a hanging-file unit with a series of labelled envelope folders to hold information.

When you go to put your paper away, if there is no file for it, make one. Put a date on the file stating when it can be thrown away. Systematically cull your files of old paperwork. Most of what we file away we don't look at. You only really look at 20 per cent of your papers regularly. Keep the files that you use most often in an accessible place.

Eliminating E-mails

Treat all your e-mails in the same ruthless way as your incoming paper. This is particularly true for ExecuMums, who will undoubtedly be inundated with e-mails.

- Check your e-mails only at set times each day (turn off your new-mail flag).
- For each mail ask, 'Can I do it, delegate it, or delete it?'
- For mail you want to store and action later, create a virtual storage system. Create labelled electronic files and folders to store your e-mails, just as you do your paper. Some possible folder titles might be: Action, Action Pending, a file for each month of the year to be examined at the start of each month, a series of alphabetical client, project or information files.
- Add electronic flags to e-mails you want to find quickly.

- Your in-box is the equivalent of your in-tray – empty it every day. Make sure you have somewhere logical to put all the files. Of course use the delete button ruthlessly.

In-trays and Daily Diaries for Kids

Why not extend the in-tray system to your children? When they bring a note home, ask them to put it straight in your in-tray.

Give each child over the age of five an envelope to act as an in-tray for them, and get them used to the idea and into the habit of dealing with it each day, just like Mum. Smaller children will need some support, but start them young. For children of ten and up, show them how to use a Daily Diary.

Teach them what you've learned. If they can become more self-sufficient and responsible it'll save you time. As they enter the teen years it will be immensely beneficial for them if they know how to organize, schedule and prioritize for themselves.

In my house, each week we have a family meeting. A bit like a team meeting at work. We update each other, quickly check schedules and discuss things we need to do. We also award a little silver trophy to the 'Mitchell of the Week'. (Never won it myself, yet!)

From the Mouths of Mums:

'My daughter attends a weekly theatre group. They communicate by "pupil post". My daughter knows that for me to action any item from notes

that come home, she has to put it into my in-tray. I deal with it, putting dates in my diary and any action that I need to take, like making a costume, into my bring-forward file, to reappear at a more appropriate time. If they are going on a theatre trip I complete consent forms and put them in her envelope. She goes through this each day and actions what's in there. She knows what she has to do for the system to work. I think that it gives her a sense of responsibility and is getting her into really good time-management habits.'

Rule Eight – Live by Lists

Tool Eight – Lifesaving List-making Machine

Lists really can be life-savers. Do you ever find that you waste loads of time and energy reinventing the wheel, thinking about the same thing again and again? How many times have you made up a list of things you need to pack when you go on holiday? How many times have you thrown it away, lost or mislaid it, so next time you go on holiday the list is nowhere to be found and a new one has to be created? How many of you rewrite birthday dates from one year's diary to another? Here are some lists you might want to adopt for yourself. And where exactly are you going to keep them? File them away in a place you will be able to find them. How about under 'L' for lists in a brand-new, alphabetically sorted filing system?

Tip! *Have a file for directions to places so you can find them when you need them.*

Useful Checklists

- Holiday essentials
- The overnight stay
- Birthdays and anniversaries (look at it each month)
- Annual chores by month
- Garden jobs by month
- Christmas
- Children's chores
- Family chores

Rule Nine – Finish What You Start

Tool Nine – I've Started So I'll Finish

Always finish what you start and then tidy it away before moving on to the next thing. Now, 'finish' doesn't necessarily mean totally finish a whole job. You can complete chunks of jobs, but once your allotted task is done, put it away. If you're halfway through making Leila's costume for the school play, don't leave it lying around. Put it out of sight until you're ready to tackle it again. This will make you feel amazingly calm, and stops carnage culminating around you as the day goes on.

Rule Ten – Only Do One Thing at a Time

Tool Ten – Focus

A systematic approach requires focus. People who do one thing at a time tend to get more done. Admittedly there are occasions when you can multitask and do two things at once. For example, ironing or exercising while watching TV, pelvic-floor exercises while standing in a queue (or reading this book!). On the whole, though, it's best to bring only one thing at a time into your near focus. When we have multiple tasks in front of our face we lose focus and clarity. A bit like a computer screen with too many windows open, we start to slow down. A good plan will let you know what to be focusing on at any one time. If you need further help with mastering this technique, just watch a man for a while.

'There is time enough for everything in the course of a day if you do but one thing at once; but there is not time enough in a year if you will do two things at a time.'

(Lord Chesterfield 1694 – 1773)

Tip! Store things as close as possible to where they are needed: bath towels in the bathroom, kitchen towels in the kitchen, etc.

Getting the Family to Join In

If your children are older you will need to negotiate an agreement around their commitment to obeying the rules. Don't expect it to happen by itself.

- Secure agreement about the new routine or rule. Discuss it with your family, avoiding the Judge Dread 'I am the Law' approach. If you want your family to buy the new routines, you'll need to sell them well and get their input. As my granny used to say, 'You catch more flies with sugar than with vinegar.'
- Be clear about what is going to happen and when it is going to happen. Check that everyone understands.
- Set a date for when the new routine will commence.
- Give your family a bit of time to get used to the idea of the routine. Remind them that the routine will start next week.
- Make sure all the tools required are available. Dusters, pens, pencils, whatever equipment they will need to do the job or follow the routine.
- Provide any training. If you want them to keep their room tidy, show them what you expect, teach them how to do it. If you want them to hang up their clothes, show them how to use a hanger and how to fold properly. Don't assume they will know.

- Agree the consequences of not following the routine.
- Reward for sticking to the routine. Encourage and praise when things get done.
- To avoid disputes, write down the routine and place it where it can be seen.

So there you have it, ten ways to really revolutionize the way you run your life. Taking strategies borrowed from industry brings a whole new meaning to 'the family business'. The more systems you can implement, the more time you will have. Start by making a few changes and see what a difference it makes, not just to how much time you have, but to how you feel.

> *Tip!* *Use couscous instead of rice, potatoes or pasta. This miracle food cooks in five minutes.*

Actions for Week Five

- Identify all the jobs you could outsource. (ten minutes)
- Delegate at least two jobs. (ten minutes each with long-term payoff in time saving)
- Notice where you lose time because you have no system or procedure in place to ensure things happen smoothly. Your Drip Diagnostics Log from Week Two may help. (five minutes)
- Buy an in-tray and bring-forward files.

- Make up a routine for the two things that slow you down most and waste your time. (Up to 20 minutes each, but think of the long-term time saving)
- Prepare a plan for implementing any of the ten tools you want to integrate into your life. (ten-15 minutes)

Tip! *Put 'due dates' into your diary, bring-forward file or mobile phone: when library books are due back, when the dry cleaning can be collected, etc. You might even want to put a reminder in a couple of days before, so you have time to track down what you'll need.*

Summary

- Systems save time, it's been proven scientifically.
- Construct systems to save you time in your home and work life.
- Get a wall planner to keep track of your family.
- Clear your house, one chunk at a time.
- Blitz rooms and children's rooms – get the kids to help.
- Give all items a home. Make sure everyone knows where everything goes.
- Dispose of items left lying around.
- Outsource as many jobs as you possibly can; get leverage. Learn how to delegate tasks to others.

- Recognize what routines you have. Streamline them, then introduce more, particularly around mealtimes.
- Identify a rolling-routine schedule.
- Use checklists.
- Handle paperwork only once: do it, dump it, or delegate it.
- Use family in-trays to manage the paper coming into your house.
- Set up time-saving storage and filing systems.
- Treat e-mails in the same way as paper.
- Only bring one thing at a time into your near focus.
- Finish what you start before moving on to something else.

Tip! *Have a Word file with directions to your house to e-mail to people rather than having to give them long-winded verbal directions.*

Week Six

Put Off Procrastination

An Ode to Procrastination

With the kids in bed to the iron I head,
But my hand somehow picks up a wine glass instead,
The telephone goes,
Better answer that I suppose,
Bound to be more fun than ironing the clothes,
To be honest though, so would picking my nose,
It's Sue on the phone, she's rung for a moan,
And the run we had booked for tomorrow postponed,
I tell you what, she knows how to drone,
And three hours later I put down the phone,
On to the washer, to take out the towels?
They've been there so long, they smell like cat's bowels.
Can't face the thought of washing that's smelly,
It's a bit late for ironing, I'll just watch some telly,
Before I know it, it's time for bed,
So up the stairs I wearily tread,
Whilst also inventing a very sore head,
No time for sex, the thought fills me with dread,
I'd rather get two minutes more sleep instead.

Time Truths 1 2 3 4 5 6 7

The cost of putting things off is higher than the price of doing them

Just Do It

Procrastinate: 'to put off (an action) until later; delay'

COLLINS DICTIONARY

If you've been doing your homework, you'll be systematic, you'll be automatic, why, you'll be like greased lightning.

Well, that's the theory, but how about the practice? Be honest now, have you done everything you set out to? Are there a few little things that you're avoiding doing? Was there a system you meant to set up but didn't quite manage? If you're one of those people who look at or think about their list and then promptly ignore it, you may be suffering from a common syndrome, known as DDS, or Dirty Dish Syndrome.

Sufferers of DDS have a tendency to put things off. One of the symptoms of this affliction is severe pain, because the cost of putting things off is higher than the price of doing them in the first place. This often leads to stress, disappointment and mayhem in the sufferer's life.

DDS (Dirty Dish Syndrome)

Let me give you some of the science behind DDS. Given the opportunity to do a task, the typical sufferer will choose not to. For example, we all know that the quickest way to wash a cup is straight after we've used it. We swill it under some hot running water and it's clean. However, if we choose to place it in the sink and leave it for an indefinite period of time, ignoring it each time we walk past, it becomes more and more difficult to wash. When we finally succumb to its silent plea to be washed, instead of requiring a quick swill it necessitates industrial-strength cleaning fluids and a power hose to blast off the mould, penicillin and encrusted coffee, which are now providing a rich food source for a small (though growing) family of cockroaches which have recently moved into your kitchen.

The currency in which you pay for not taking action isn't necessarily financial. It can be accounted for in all manner of ways. In the case of the dirty cup, it's effort and time, but procrastination can cost you your health, your finances and your relationship with your family. More often than not, the things we put off are our blueberries, items which fall into the valuable but non-urgent compartment of the shopping basket of life. Put off for too long, they can lead to cost and regret.

From the Mouths of Mums:

'I knew I needed to go to the dentist and I kept putting it off until I had the most hideous toothache. I had to leave a dinner party I was at, I was in so much pain. It kept me awake all night and cost me a fortune at an emergency dental surgery the next day. I also had to cancel an important meeting.'

Think of three things that you have put off in the past. Make a list. What did it cost you to put them off?

What did I put off?	What did it cost me?

Why on Earth Do We Put Things Off?

So why do we do this? We know it doesn't make sense. We can rationalize the sensible nature of getting things done, but for some reason we still procrastinate. How bizarre. Well, I'm going to let you into a secret that not many people know. You are not completely in charge of what you are doing. You might think you are, but have you ever found that when you make a decision, some internal voice seems to challenge you and then take control? It's as if you've been possessed by someone or something. You make a decision to take action, then something inside you sabotages your good intent and you don't follow through.

Let me give you an example all mums can relate to. You're on a diet, which of course means you won't be eating cake or biscuits, doesn't it? The inevitable happens: there's a huge piece of chocolate cake left over at a child's birthday party.

Yikes, someone offers it to you. Consciously you know what you want to say. You want to say, 'No thanks,' but a little voice of influence comes from somewhere inside you, and the word 'Yes' comes out of your mouth. Before you know it, that slice of cake you'd consciously decided not to eat has tingled your tastebuds and somehow found its way into the depths of your stomach. It's now slowly working its way towards your hips. How on earth did that happen? Simple – as I said, you're not totally in charge of your decision-making.

You are influenced by something from within that makes your hand reach out and take the cake.

Your Internal Management Team

Some people like to call this internal influence their Inner Voice. Some people call it their Gremlin or Demon. I call mine my Time-Management Team, or my TMT. My Time-Management Team has various players, with differing voices.

These voices influence me. They make me lie in bed when I know I should get up. They stop me from telling my boss I'm going home on time. They make me eat chocolate cake when I know I don't need it. They, not me, sometimes seem to run my life. That needs to change.

You need to take charge of your Time-Management Team, because after all, it is your life. Everybody is different and their team has different members. I've asked many people about the influences that prevent them from getting on with what they need to do. What

I've discovered is that there seems to be a common theme around the members of the Team. So, let's meet them and see if you recognize anybody.

Fanny Fun

Fanny just wants to have fun. Why would you make the children's beds when you could be out having coffee instead? 'Come on,' she'll say, 'just watch a few more minutes of the chat show, the dishes can wait.' Why would you finish off that urgent report when you could be in the meeting about the office Christmas party? The only thing she wants in her near focus is fun.

The Terrible Twins: Do it Later Delia and Complacent Camilla

Delia and Camilla will assure you that you have plenty of time to do it later. Everything is under control. Why would you worry about Christmas in June? That presentation you've got to give is weeks away. You'll have plenty of time nearer the day.

Do those things that are right in your focus now. That other stuff can wait a while.

Stella Stress

She'll have you convinced that it's best to put as much off as possible, because of course you do your best work under pressure. When the chips are down and you're really up against it, you produce amazing results. A bit of stress is good for you, isn't it? Keep everything out of your near focus until the very last minute.

Hilda Habit

Are there lots of little things that you always put off? What little habits does Hilda hold you to before you start work? For example, do you always have a coffee? Do all your pencils need to be sharpened? Do you have to check your e-mails (again)? Do you habituate towards procrastination or away from it? If you feel like you're hurtling towards it at 100mph, then it is likely Hilda Habit is hard at work. Bless her cotton socks. She'll have you procrastinating like you don't know what, and you won't even have to think about it. The only things she wants in her near focus are things she's used to.

Linda Lazy

Quite honestly, Linda Lazy can't be bothered to get anything done. Everything's too much effort. Come on, the strain of climbing out of your comfort zone is just too much. Stay where you are, do nothing, it's much easier. Her motto: 'No gain, no pain.' The only thing she wants in her near focus is anything to make her life easy.

The Gruesome Twosome: Freda Fear and Patricia Perfection

Patricia wants everything to be perfect, and Freda is frightened of failing. Between them, they'll persuade you to put things off until the last minute. That way you won't have time to do anything properly. Then, of course, you've got a fabulous excuse for failure and for not reaching perfection. What a team. They don't want anything in their near focus until it's too late to do it properly, giving them an excuse for not doing a great job.

Nina No-time

Overwhelmed by the sheer size of any task, Nina will look at it and categorically tell you that there isn't enough time to get it all done. Leave it until a day when you do have plenty of time, she'll suggest. We all know a day like that is as likely as snow in the desert. To justify herself Nina will direct your attention to all the little, less important jobs you have to do. By bringing these into your near focus, Nina will make you feel like you're really busy. But we all know you're busy doing nothing all day long. Well, nothing of any importance anyway.

Clarissa Can't Do

Clarissa will look at any task and tell you point-blank, 'You can't do it.' Whether it's a tax return, putting up a picture hook or making a flambé, she'll convince you that it can't be done by you, so best put it off. Bring something you can do into your near focus.

Who's Running Your Team?

These characters all have fabulous powers of persuasion, and who are you to argue with them? How about you're the boss? You have to take charge. If you don't, it'll end up costing you dear. All the members of your team mean well, and they are on your side, but they're misguided. They are all trying to help and protect you. Fanny is protecting you from boredom, Freda and Patricia from the embarrassment of failure, and Linda from over-straining yourself. The question is, do you need their protection? Do the benefits of putting things off outweigh the benefits of doing them right now? I know that I sometimes feel as if not doing things saves me time. In the short term it usually does, but in the long term it usually doesn't.

Think of a few things you're avoiding. Use the Table of Temptation on the next page to analyse the pros and cons of your personal procrastination.

Tip! *Keep a notebook and pen next to your bed so if you have any great ideas you can write them down and get to sleep. If a worry is keeping you awake, give it the same treatment.*

The Table of Temptation

What am I putting off?	Why am I avoiding it?	Benefit of putting it off	Benefit of doing it now	What am I tempted to do?
Dental visit.	I'm too busy to fit it in.	I will have more time right now to do other things that I really need to do.	I will have significantly more time in the future. It is less likely to impact negatively on my schedule in the longer term. Dental health is linked to life expectancy. I will avoid hideous tooth-ache and live longer.	OK, OK, I know I've got to book my dental appointment right this minute.
Finding a part-time job.	Lack of confidence fuelled by fear of failure.	I can't fail if I don't try. It's easier not to bother. Things stay as they are.	I'll have more money. I'll get out of the house. Find new friends. Get some variety in my life. Feel more fulfilled.	OK, OK, I'll take a small step and call for an application form.

Top-20 Put-offs

Listed below are 20 typical reasons why people procrastinate. Work your way down the list noting the ones that seem to apply to you. Then take a look at the Procrastination Busters to help you put off procrastination and get a move on with the things that matter to you.

1. I don't fancy doing the task in hand.
2. The task takes too long.
3. I haven't got time to finish the task, so I won't start.
4. There's something more appealing than doing this task.
5. This task will take too much effort.
6. I don't think I can complete this task perfectly.
7. A little voice in my head says do this task later.
8. The deadline is way off so I'll do it later.
9. I do things better under pressure.
10. Excuses: I'm too tired, I'm too stressed, I'm too fat, the children stop me.
11. The task seems too big to contemplate.
12. I don't have time.
13. The task is in my blind spot.
14. I don't know how to do this task.
15. I've already got too much to do.
16. I don't have a plan.
17. What if I do this task and I fail?

18. Putting things off is just the way I am.
19. The circumstances aren't right for beginning this task.
20. The task is not urgent.

What Are You Putting Off?

Think about all the things that you are putting off right now. Make a list. (Please don't say you'll do it later!)

-
-
-
-
-
-
-

For each item, work out what's stopping you from doing it, then try out the Procrastination Buster that goes with your put-off.

Top-Ten Procrastination Busters

Here are ten Procrastination Busters to help you transform your Time-Management Team voices into your Dream Team.

Select the put-offs you use most regularly from the left-hand column. Then try out the procrastination-busting solutions from one to ten, identified in the top row. Solutions numbered one, six and ten are like aspirin – they're good for any problem.

Use those first and, if the procrastination persists, go straight to the heart of the problem with the targeted solution identified for that issue.

Tip! Put your clothes straight into the washing basket rather than getting there via the floor, where they have a tendency to gang up and loiter with intent.

Procrastination Buster One: Crystal Balls

Have you ever wished that you had a crystal ball so you could see into your future? Using the power of neurotechnology (your brain!) I'll show you how to do it. Like Ebenezer Scrooge and the Ghost of Christmas Yet to Come, when you become a voyeur of your own fate you'll see the consequences of your current actions. When we procrastinate we make a decision in the present moment not to focus on something. These decisions create our future.

Remember the definition of time:

'The continuous passage of existence in which events pass from a state of potentiality in the future, through the present, to a state of finality in the past.'

The Crystal Balls technique allows you to view the potential of future events and gives you a chance to reconsider what you focus on in the present. So, just

SOLUTIONS

	1. Crystal Balls	2. Reframing	3. Bite of the Apple	4. Volume Control	5. Can't Do to Can Do	6. No Pudding for Procrastinators	7. Inject Urgency	8. New Habits	9. It Needn't Be Perfect	10. Management Meetings
I don't fancy doing the task in hand.	X	X				X				X
The task takes too long.	X	X		X		X			X	X
I haven't got time to finish the task, so I won't start.	X		X			X				X
There's something more appealing than doing this task.	X	X				X				X
This task will take too much effort.	X	X	X			X				X
I don't think I can complete this task perfectly.	X				X	X			X	X
A little voice in my head says do this task later.	X			X		X				X

The deadline is way off so I'll do it later.	X					X	X			X
I do things better under pressure.	X					X	X	X		X
Excuses: I'm too tired, too stressed, too fat, the children stop me.	X					X				X
The task seems too big to contemplate.	X		X			X				X
I don't have time.	X		X			X				X
The task is in my blind spot.	X					X				X
I don't know how to do this task.	X				X	X				X
I've already got too much to do.	X		X			X				X
I don't have a plan.	X		X			X				X
What if I do this task and I fail?	X					X		X		X
Putting things off is just the way I am.	X					X		X		X
The circumstances aren't right for beginning this task.	X	X				X				X
The task is not urgent.	X					X	X			X

like Scrooge, you too can change your ways and create the future of your choosing.

From the Mouths of Mums:

'I struggle to find the time to fit in my computer course. I'm tempted to give up, but I know it will help get me back into the workplace when the children go to school. I can see a time in the future when I'll be doing book-keeping from home if I stick at it.'

'When I really don't feel like dealing with a pile of washing, in my imagination I take myself to tomorrow and think about how much worse it will look then, and how much worse I will feel. I then think about how it will look and how I will feel if I just do it now. It helps to motivate me into action.'

Tip! *Use your answering machine – you don't always have to answer the phone just because it's ringing!*

Gaze into Your Fabulous Future

This may seem a little strange at first, but I've used this technique many times and it really helps to get you moving. To look into your future, you must first know where it is, so we're going to locate it. Stand in a space with no other people around. If I asked you to gaze into your future, where would you look? Many people think that their future is out in front of them, their past is behind them, and where they are standing right now represents their present. What about you, where do you think your past, present and future are?

- Look in the direction of where you think your future is, then point to it. Notice where you are pointing. Notice how far away your future goes from you. Like the gold dust in your egg timer, how much do you think you've got left?
- Point to your past. Notice where you are pointing, notice how far away from you your past goes.
- Point to your present. Notice where you are pointing. Are you standing in your present, is it high up, low down, in front of you, to the side, does it go around you? Really notice where it seems to start and end, in relation to the future and the past.
- Get yourself a pen and a paper and make a drawing of what you have just done. An art degree is not required. Draw yourself as a stick woman, then draw a line which connects the past, present and future together just like a dot-to-dot. If your line seems wiggly, make it wiggly; if it wraps around you, wrap it around you; if it goes to the side of you, draw it to the side of you. It might be going over your head, it might go from front to back or side to side. There is no right or wrong, just draw.

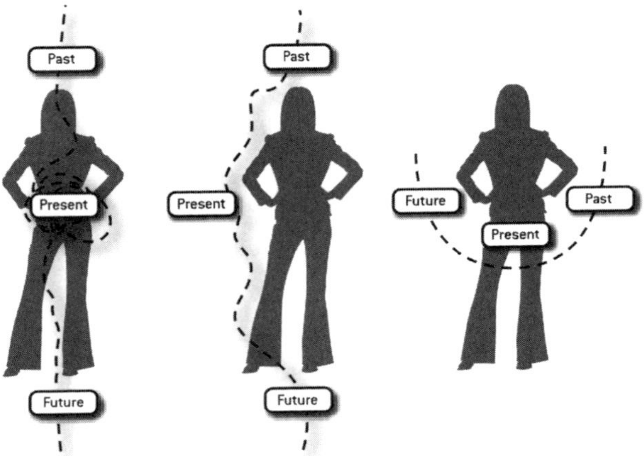

Typical Time Lines

Tip! *Do you really need to bathe slightly older children every night?!*

What you've drawn is your Time Line, and as you stand in your present gazing along it into your future, you become like a human crystal ball, able to see the consequences of your actions. By bringing the consequences of not taking action into our present consciousness, it helps us take the right action.

Often we put things off because the consequences of not doing them are too far into the future. The feedback is too far into the future. The instant gratification of putting something off outweighs the small but instant pain of doing it now.

Something like smoking is a perfect example of delayed feedback. In the present moment any smoker could influence their future by making a decision to stop smoking. We all know that the after-effects of this habit can take years to appear, and the instant pleasure a smoker derives from a cigarette overrides the far-off future consequences. You need to get present with the consequences of the decisions and choices you are making. Use the Crystal Ball of Crisis and the Crystal Ball of Compulsion to see the future effects of choosing to put things off.

The Crystal Ball of Crisis

- Think of one thing you've been putting off. Maybe it's spending real quality time with your children. Maybe it's exercise, or finding a new job.
- Look into your future. What do you see in a week, in a month, in six months, a year, five years, ten years? Take a moment to really see, hear and feel the experience of a 'you' in the future, living with the consequences of the actions that you put off now.
- What do you see at the end of your life if you keep putting this off?
- However bad this seems, make the pictures, feelings and sounds you experience out in the future ten times worse.
- Bring yourself back to the present.

The Crystal Ball of Compulsion

- Think again about the action you've been putting off. Imagine that you have decided to do it. For example, you will spend some real quality time with your children, you will exercise or you will move jobs.

- Look into your future. What do you see in a week, in a month, in six months, a year, five years, ten years?
- What do you see at the end of your life, if you take this action now?
- Take a moment to really see, hear and feel the experience of a 'you' in the future, living with the positive consequences of doing what you've been putting off.
- However good this seems, make the pictures, feelings and sounds you experience out in the future ten times better.

Compare the two future pictures, the one of crisis and the one of compulsion. Now make a decision about what to do in the moment. Hopefully this will encourage you to make more empowered decisions when tempted to put something off. Give yourself a choice before making a decision about what to focus on. Remember that the one and only place you can affect your future is in the here and now, the present. What you choose to do today will shape your life tomorrow. Make the right choice or you'll live with the consequences.

Procrastination Buster Two: Reframing

The way we look at tasks can affect how we feel about them, and subsequently whether we do them or not.

Fanny Fun will see tasks as boring, Linda Lazy as too much effort, and Nina No-time as too big. Sometimes, though, looking at a task in a different way can give us the impetus we need to get started. If you are resisting doing a task, ask yourself: how can I look at this differently so the resistance will be removed?

Let's take Fanny Fun as an example. For her to be satisfied you need to make whatever you're doing fun. If it happens to be clearing out the garage, how could you make that fun? Could you play loud music? Could you have a garage-clearing party? How could you turn this around to overcome Fanny's objections? With Nina No-time, how could you reframe the large task of garage-cleaning? Take a moment to chunk it down into a series of smaller tasks, so it's no longer a large one. What's in it for Linda Lazy? Could the garage-cleaning be reframed as an opportunity to clear some space for a sunbed in the corner? She can lazily lie on that to her heart's content. Whatever resistance you're experiencing, look at the task another way. See if it helps.

Tip! *Train everyone in your family never to put anything down but to put it away.*

From the Mouths of Mums:

'This is shocking, but I hated changing my son's nappies. Often I'd think, "I'll do it later." Then I decided to change my focus and think about this

activity not as nappy-changing but as a bonding session, a chance to play and have some fun one-on-one time. I have to say it did help, and I didn't feel so guilty either.'

'I found playing with my children a bit boring, so avoided it even though I told myself that I really wanted to do it. Instead of thinking of myself as a boring mum, I thought of myself as a magician, as a magical person. Thinking of myself in this different light helped me to play in a more engaged, fun way with the children, and the playing wasn't boring.'

Procrastination Buster Three: Bite of the Apple

Faced with a huge task it's easy to feel daunted. As mums we rarely have huge chunks of time, just snatched bits and pieces here and there. So where do you start with those mammoth tasks that take too long and seem so huge? Well, like eating an apple, banana or an elephant, you tackle these things one bite at a time. You engage in the activity known as long-term planning and time-chunking. In Week Four we looked at how you break down larger goals into more manageable tasks. We used the Three Magic Questions to break goals down into chunks:

1. What do I need to do?
2. When do I need to do it by?
3. What else do I need to do?

We assigned Destiny Dates and learned how to transfer them into the Daily Diary. This is a great technique. Another easy way of getting you started on a large task that you're resisting is to just do one small thing towards it. Do one thing today that will start you on the journey of completing the task.

From the Mouths of Mums:

'I needed to decide which school to send my daughter to. It seemed like a huge task with so many to choose from, and I kept putting it off. To make myself take action I asked the question, "What could I do today to make this happen?" As a first step I made just one five-minute phone call to get a list of all the local schools.

It felt like a good first move and made me feel better. My next step was to shortlist the schools, and so it went on, until the task was finally complete. But each day I asked myself the question, "What can I do today to help me complete this task?"'

Take a large task you've been putting off and ask yourself this question: 'What can I do today to help me complete this task?'

Each journey of a thousand steps begins with a single step. Taking even a baby step will move you closer to your goals. It'll motivate you to take more action as you start to gain momentum.

Here's an example of a typical 'mission impossible': revamping a child's bedroom. By setting a realistic deadline and by breaking the tasks down into smaller chunks, the impossible becomes possible.

Each time you complete a small step, use the Crystal Ball technique to imagine that the project is finished. Look out into the future using your crystal ball and Time Line. In your mind's eye, see, hear and feel what this project will be like when it is complete. (This is also a great technique to motivate children into action.) As you look at the completed project, give yourself a little affirmation for success. An affirmation is a short positive statement that lets you know you are moving in the right direction. Think of one for yourself, write it down and look at it each day to remind yourself that you are making progress and to motivate you further. Here's an example of an affirmation:

'Every day I am getting closer and closer to achieving all the tasks that are really important to me and make a significant difference in my life.'

Procrastination Buster Four: Volume Control

Do you find that you're having conversations in your head over the pros and cons of getting on with something? Does your Management Team provide a constant source of banter in your brain that's leaving you with a headache? Do they persuade you to procrastinate? If so,

Mission Possible: Sort Emma's Room
Completion: 3 weeks from today (= 21 March)

Task name and order	Time to complete	Date due	Dele-gated	Date done
Clear floor and sort drawers	1 hour	5 March	Emma	3 March
Sort wardrobe and desk	2 hours	9 March	Emma	6 March
Sort clothes by size/season	1 hour	9 March	Emma/ Mum	7 March
Label clothes to reuse and put in bag in loft	1 hour	9 March	Mum	9 March
Recycle old clothes	30 mins	10 March	Dad	15 March
Get new shelving	30 mins when out shopping	8 March	Dad	15 March
Buy new coat hangers	20 mins when out shopping	8 March	Dad	15 March
Buy containers for toys	20 mins when out shopping	8 March	Dad	10 March
Throw away broken toys and sort toys into categories	1 hour	10 March	Mum/ Emma	10 March
Buy pots for pens, pencils and equipment	30 mins when out shopping	13 March	Mum/ Emma	10 March
Choose paint samples	30 mins when out shopping	8 March	Mum	5 March
Choose paint colour	45 minutes	10 March	Mum/ Emma	7 March
Buy paint	20 mins when out shopping	13 March	Dad	15 March
Prepare room for painting	1 hour	14 March	Mum/ Emma	14 March
Paint room and put up shelves	1 weekend	Booked – 15/16 March	Grandpa	16 March
Sort out room post-painting	1 hour	16 March	Mum/ Emma	16 March
Bottle of buck's fizz to celebrate	As long as you like	16 March	Every-one	16 March

learn how to use your own personal volume control to turn down the torturous tones of the tongues that tempt you, and say no to their nagging.

- Identify where the voice in your head comes from. Is it the front, the back, the left or the right, inside or outside your head? Are you being seduced in stereo or just in one ear?
- Acknowledge the voice. Recognize that it is trying to help you.
- Imagine you have a volume control on the side of your head.
- Using the control, in your mind just turn down the voice that you don't want to listen to. If it's Do It Later Delia or Freda Fear, make a conscious choice to listen to the voice of influence that supports you in taking action and turn the others down.

Use your new-found control to turn down the volume on unwanted feelings, too. Notice when you are feeling under pressure, stressed or guilty, for example. None of these emotions is terribly helpful for productivity, so whenever you become aware of them use your volume control and turn them down. If on the off-chance you happen to be feeling productive, use your control knob to turn that up. See how much more you get done. Use this to help you focus on what you want. Put the rest into a blind – or in this case a deaf – spot.

Procrastination Buster Five: Can't Do to Can Do

It's a real cop-out, isn't it, 'I can't do it'? If you say it often enough, then you'll really believe it. Remember your RAS? The response unit to the brain that looks for what you want in life? Tell it you can't do something and it will be in overdrive looking for evidence to support that belief. As Henry Ford famously said, *'If you think you can do a thing or think you can't do a thing, you're right.'*

So if you find yourself agreeing with Clarissa Can't Do as she categorically calls out 'You can't', here's the antidote. Try these really simple ways to get you thinking that you can. Then guess what? You probably will.

When working with people who tell me they can't do things, I ask them to consider their dilemma in a different way. I encourage them to rephrase their 'can't-do' belief into a statement of future possibility. Here's how:

- Question your 'can't-do' belief by asking yourself the following question: 'Is it that I really can't do it, or is it that I just don't know how?' I know I can't play the piano, but it's only because I don't know how.
- Open up to the possibility that this is something you could achieve in the future. Instead of saying, 'I can't do it', say, 'I can't do it yet.' This also gives you permission to move forward.

- Ask, 'What would I need to know, learn, or do, to be able to do this?' and
- Imagine yourself doing this thing you can't do yet at some point in the future. See, hear and feel what it's like to be doing your 'can't-do'.

Ask yourself:
What steps did I take to achieve this?
What options did I have and which ones did I choose?
What did I do to motivate myself to get on with it?
Who helped me?
What is it like achieving this?
Where would I be now if I had chosen not to do this?
What action will I take today to move forward with this can't-do and transform it into a can-do?

Come on, kick your legs up and start dancing the cancan.

Procrastination Buster Six: No Pudding for Procrastinators

If you're struggling to muster motivation, then give yourself a reward when the task is complete. It's a bit like telling the children they can't have pudding until they've eaten their main course. You only give yourself pudding when procrastination is off your personal menu. If you motivate yourself to complete a task that you really didn't want to do, celebrate and reward yourself. I'm sure you don't need me to give you a million suggestions for personal reward. You're more than capable of thinking of a few things.

Procrastination Buster Seven: Inject Urgency

When people tell me they do things better when they're under pressure, I know we're in for trouble. It reliably informs me that, finding themselves in a burning building, they only run when the flames are about to lick their bum. It's just not healthy to live like this. Here are some tips for avoiding this type of pressure:

- Create pressure artificially. Bring your deadline forward and give yourself breathing space.
- Make a plan with contingency built in – and stick to it. Always add between ten and 20 per cent extra buffer time to give you some room for manoeuvre. When you get into the habit of completing things on time or even early, you'll never want to go back.
- Get someone else to hold you accountable. You might decide to put all your photos into albums by Christmas. Ask a friend to check in with you periodically, at set dates before the deadline, to see if you've done what you said you would.
- Build in milestones that will force you to do small parts of the task on a regular basis. For example, by July have Lucy, Lauren and Kit's baby photos all put away.

Tip! *Focus on one thing at a time. When you try to catch two rabbits, they both get away.*

From the Mouths of Mums

'I am absolutely terrible at leaving things until the last minute. To get better at this I have started putting things into my diary earlier than I need to. I'm also trying to be more realistic about how long things take. Last year I was up until 1am wrapping my daughter's birthday presents and getting her party ready. Why? I thought I'd have time, and I like a bit of pressure, but to be honest it took all the fun out of it. I was really tired on the big day. It was nobody's fault but my own. Next year everything will be ready a week in advance so I can enjoy the event.'

Procrastination Buster Eight: New Habits

We often put things off because we've just got into the habit of putting them off. We all have things we habitually say, think or do, which have the equivalent impact on our productivity as shooting ourselves in the foot – ouch! Our motivation wanes as bad procrastination habits hold us back. Well, I'm pleased to tell you, you don't have to be a nun to get a new habit.

From the Mouths of Mums:

'I have this really annoying habit of always feeling that I have to check my e-mails just

before I leave the office. I also want to get home to see the kids. I'm pulled in two directions, and the e-mails always seem to triumph. When I realized that this was just a bad habit that I'd got into, I put some structures in place to help me get home on time. I told the children I would be home at 6.30. I made a commitment to myself to get out of the office on time. I had my mobile phone sound an alarm at 5.40 to remind me that it was time to wind down and prepare for the next day. I scheduled three small blocks of time during the day to deal with e-mails. Each day I successfully got home on time, I'd get my kids to put a big red tick on our wall planner. It did help me create a new habit.'

Tip! *Leave the lid off your washing tablet box, so you can just reach in and get what you need.*

How to Create a New Habit

- Decide what new habit you want. For example, going to bed at a reasonable time.
- Identify what triggers your old habitual behaviour. In this case maybe it's all the bits and pieces lying around that distract you and stop you from going to bed because you deal with those instead. Maybe it's watching telly.
- Think of ways to remove the trigger. When I was tempted to read the local newspaper's property

section every Friday rather than get on with my work, I decided that the best way to eliminate the trigger was to cancel the paper. It worked. I couldn't read it because it wasn't there!

- Create a structure to support your new habit. Some examples are: make a tick-list for the next 21 days to monitor your progress. This will also help you to be mindful of your new behaviour. Put a reminder note on your wall, wear a particular piece of jewellery to trigger thoughts of action. Put a reminder in your Daily Diary. Remember, people who write their intentions down are more likely to manifest them.
- Celebrate your success and reward yourself.

Tip! *Put your photographs into albums as soon as you get them. Don't wait until you have 5,000 all out of order and have lost the will even to try to sort them out. Work through the backlog a small chunk at a time.*

From the Mouths of Mums:

'I was always saying to my children, "I'll read you a story in a minute." The minute never came and neither did the story. In fact, I realized that I'd got into a dreadful habit of constantly saying, "Just a minute, I'll do it in a minute." I decided that I needed to change this. I put a

Post-it note on the kitchen cupboard by the kettle. It said, "A story a day keeps guilt away." Then, every time I had a coffee, I sat down and made it story time. This became my new habit, but it took a bit of effort at first.'

Procrastination Buster Nine: It Needn't Be Perfect

When we set ourselves the standard of perfection, is it any wonder we put things off? With such a high bar to reach, we're likely to fail. When the inevitable happens and we aren't successful, we beat ourselves up and decide to put more things off because we don't want to experience further failure. It becomes a vicious downward spiral. The question to ask yourself is this, 'Does everything really have to be perfect? What would be an acceptable standard?' Why not take a leaf from the book of Italian economist Vilfredo Pareto, who developed the 80/20 principle. The 80/20 Law states that 20 per cent of your efforts will produce 80 per cent of your results. After that you get diminishing returns on your effort and focus. If you're a brain surgeon or the director of a nuclear power plant, then I agree, the need for perfection is justified, but in every component of our lives do we need such high standards?

The irony is, because we put things off we consequently don't leave enough time to do them properly anyway. We then give ourselves a real dose of stress in our attempts to do our best in limited time. And what if you do fail? Does it really matter? Every successful person will tell you that they have failed at one time or another. The difference is they don't think of their failure as failure. They reframe it and think about it as feedback. They learn something so that they can improve their performance next time.

In his efforts to invent the lightbulb, Thomas Edison failed hundreds of times. He never saw this as such. Each failure was a step forward to finding the right solution. He reframed the experience as one of learning. He knew what not to do on his next attempt. Imagine if he'd given up because he didn't reach perfection first time. We'd have no electric lightbulbs, no electric dishwashers and, perish the thought, no electric hair straighteners today. No, no, don't even think about it, perfection does not have to be the pinnacle, your best will do.

Five Questions to Ask Yourself When Patricia Perfectionist Is at Work

1. What would happen if this wasn't perfect?
2. If I just did my best what would I have to do?
3. How much less effort would it take to reach a perfectly acceptable standard?
4. Who says this has to be perfect?
5. What will happen if I attempt to reach perfection?

Five Ways to turn Fear of Failure into Courage

1. List the benefits of achieving what you're putting off.

2. Ask yourself, 'What's the worst thing that could possibly happen if I have a go?'
3. Ask yourself, 'What's the best thing that could possibly happen if I have a go?'
4. Take inspiration from others who have failed but persevered in order to reach their goals.
5. Think of three ways that attempting this could make you stronger as a person.

If you achieve all your dreams and desires without ever failing, then you've not tried hard enough, or dreamt hard enough.

Procrastination Buster Ten: Management Meetings

When the team in your head is giving you a million excuses not to do what you need to do, sit down and have a meeting with them. I did this exercise once with a client over the phone. She was in an office, which unbeknown to me had glass walls. My advice is to do this where people can't see or hear you. They will think you have become insane, but believe me, daft as it looks, it's really effective.

- Put out two chairs that face each other. When you sit in one chair you will represent the views of yourself. You will put the case forward for getting on with the job in hand. In the other chair you will represent the case of your team – Hilda

Habit, Fanny Fun, Freda Fear and the rest of the gang, who want to put things off.

- Start by sitting in chair one. State all the reasons for getting on with the job: 'We won't get stressed later, it will save time in the long run, I'm fed up with this job hanging around all the time,' etc, etc.
- Move to the second chair and state the reasons from your Management Team for putting the job off. Your Management Team will have a plethora of reasons, many of them identified earlier in this chapter.
- Return to the first chair and explain to the team all the reasons why their justifications are not valid. Tell them the benefits of doing the job now, in particular what's specifically in it for them.
- Come to a compromise with your Management Team, so everyone is happy and you can take action to move forward.

Have fun with this. How silly are some of the arguments?

So there you have it, 10 procrastination busters. There's always a reason why we could put something off. If you want to live the life of your choosing, take control of what you do in the moment and tomorrow will be surprisingly fabulous.

Tip! *Make meals in bulk, then freeze them in portions to use another day.*

Actions for Week Six

- Look at your list of things you've been putting off. (five minutes)
- Choose two of them to work on this week. One should be a small, achievable item – for example, spending ten minutes every day playing one-on-one with your children. It could be putting up a picture that's been propped against the wall for months. The other should be a larger, more time-consuming project.
- Totally complete the small item. (five-20 minutes)
- Break the larger task down into manageable chunks. Put all the short-term actions into your Daily Diary. (ten minutes)
- Take at least one step on the larger project. (five-20 minutes.) Remember, lots of small steps will move you forward.
- Don't put it off. Put the book down and start now!

Summary

- We have a tendency to put things off.
- The long-term cost of putting something off is usually greater than the short-term price of just doing it in the first place.
- We are influenced to put things off by our internal thoughts. We can learn how to overcome these influences.

- The usual reason for procrastination is that we see a benefit in the moment for doing so. The short-term gain often seems more appealing than the long-term consequences.
- To put an end to procrastination, we can learn new habits and techniques around taking action.

Tip! *Put labels on everything. If something goes missing, it will be returned as if by magic.*

Week Seven

Human Doing to Human Being

An Ode to Savouring Time

When you were born, I felt so forlorn,
'Cos all you did was squawk,
All I could do was long for the day,
When you would begin to talk,
A word or a phrase, for which I could give praise,
And when would you start to walk?
Not satisfied then, I still wanted more,
When would you be four?
So school we'd explore,
And wouldn't it be great,
When you got to be eight,
We'd take you to restaurants with real china plates,
And what would come next?
I could teach you to text,
On turning 13 you'd be a teen queen,
Mum and Dad no longer your scene.
On hitting 18,
Off our hands what a dream,
But now I am old, and my house is so cold,
Not full of chaos and kids I must scold,
Those wonderful years, full of laughter and tears,
Oh why did I wish them away?

Time Truths 1 2 3 4 5 6 7

If you can live
in the moment
you can expand
time

Are You a Doing or a Being?

If you have read thus far, and implemented what you've learned, chances are you've been transformed into a lean, mean doing machine. You value your time. You know how you spend it and you've been the proud instigator of plans and systems that have licked your life into shape. You, yes you, are getting everything done.

This alone will leave you feeling fantastic about your Time Management, your life management and your relationship with yourself. But don't close the book just yet. There is more. You still have to hear about the icing on the cake. You're going to learn how to make every moment magical. Yes, you read correctly, *how to make every moment magical.*

As mums our focus is very much on doing, on completing tasks, on nourishing and nurturing others. More often than not we do this within tightly set time-parameters and find ourselves rushing through life. Our brains are whizzing ahead, constantly thinking about what has to be done next. We're distracted by thoughts of what to cook for tea, while doing William's reading, and what to say in the client meeting, while bathing Morgan. In the midst of our organizing and doing, we sometimes forget to just enjoy ourselves, to just be, to savour the moment. We neglect to nourish ourselves and our souls. In short, we don't focus on living as human beings. Have you become a human doing?

From the Mouths of Mums:

'I'm not too bad at getting things done, but I never really feel like I'm fully engaged in what I'm doing. I'm always thinking or worrying about what has to happen next.'

RQT: Real Quality Time

With the systems, structures and planning processes you've put in place, tasks will more easily take care of themselves. With 'doing' out of the way, you can move your focus towards 'being'. In a state of being you can expand time by totally immersing yourself in every moment. You can also start to make more of your quality time. In today's demanding society people don't just want more time, they want RQT – real quality time – and why not? How fabulous would it be to live your life making every moment matter, to live life with zest? It's a skill many of us have forgotten.

I was totally amazed by an article I read recently about a training course in Germany. Here, stressed-out parents are taught how to relax, release their inner child and make sand castles before they go on holiday. Enjoying themselves on a family break is something they've seemingly forgotten how to do. Get the hang of living in the moment and you'll be experiencing not just quality time, but RQT, real quality time, on a regular basis. Thankfully, no German happy-clappy camps required for you.

For many mothers the notion of just 'being' and enjoying RQT is totally fanciful. I've come across people who can't even picture themselves having RQT. Often, mothers of small children tell me that they literally drag themselves through the day.

They dream about their children going to bed. In stark contrast I have worked with mothers who have regrets about not properly savouring the time they had with their children when they were little. They say that when their children were small, time seemed to drag. With hindsight, the time seems to have gone really quickly. An odd contradiction, yet time does tend to play these tricks on us. So how can you make the most of every moment? What can you do so that when you look back in years to come your life will seem like a rich tapestry of wonderful experiences that you were able to savour?

Time Is Like a Box of Chocolates

In true *Forrest Gump* style I like to think about time like a box of chocolates. If you get given a box of chocs, how do you eat them? Do you wolf them down like a dog or do you eat them slowly and savour every tantalizing mouthful? If you were to think about time like chocolate, are you gulping it down and rushing through it? Or are you savouring every minute?

Understanding your own natural tendencies when it comes to the way you devour time will ultimately determine your ability to savour it. Most people have never spent a second thinking about how they perceive time. We all perceive it differently and have different relationships with it. Take a moment to think about how you connect with time.

Exercise – Just a Minute

Use a digital watch, or have someone keep time for you. Close your eyes and open them when you think a minute has passed. (No counting elephants in your head please!) See if you know how long a minute is. Do you open your eyes too soon? Did your minute seem to take a long time to pass? If so, maybe you're rushing through other things, too. Let this give you an idea of how well your body clock is calibrated with time.

Are You in a Good State or a Right State?

Our baseline state is a bit like our resting heart rate; it's how we are most of the time. It can change depending on what we are doing, but this is the baseline we always come back to. How are you most of the time? What is your way of being? You only need to look at people to get a feeling for their baseline state. Some people do things faster – walking, breathing, talking – while others do things more slowly.

Your baseline state will affect how you interact with time and how you calibrate with your environment. Think for a moment: how do you tend to move, think and feel most of the time? Do you usually feel at one with your activities and environment? Or is your state not conducive to this? Look at the statements below to give you a feel for how well you're calibrated with time.

Things to Make You Go Ummm

Put a tick next to the statement on the left or right that seems most like you.

I tend to do things at a fast pace.	I tend to do things in a measured way.
I quite often have feelings of guilt about what I'm not doing.	I don't tend to feel guilty about what I don't achieve.
I find it difficult to switch off sometimes, I'm always thinking about the day's events.	I am able to switch off and focus on the task in hand.
I tend to have lots of things on the go at once.	I do one thing at a time.
I can get emotional and worked up.	I tend to be more factual than emotional.
I always think I've got more time than I have; things take me longer than I planned.	I have a good sense of how long things will take.
I'm always telling myself and others how little time I have.	I don't go on and on about having no time.
I'm easily distracted from what I am doing.	I'm not easily distracted.
The days, weeks and years seem to roll into one.	Time seems to be spaced out nicely and running at a good pace.
Sometimes when I am with the children or at work, the day seems to drag.	I enjoy my time, even the mundane things aren't too bad.

The more ticks you have in the left-hand side, the more likely you still have a lot of Manic Martha about you. Although you may be getting many things done, you probably aren't savouring what you do. I'll always remember at my wedding, the best man, my lovely brother-in-law, finished his speech with the wise words of Walter Hagen:

'Don't hurry, don't worry, and don't forget to smell the flowers along the way.'

Have you stopped to stick your nose in any big blooms lately? Or are you travelling so fast you're trampling over every flower bed in sight?

Conversely, if you have more ticks on the right-hand side, you're more like Perfect Paula. With a clear head and a sense of direction you know everything's sorted for the future and will happen because you've planned it that way. You can set the scene for days where you can focus on just enjoying each moment as it comes.

What Prevents You from Savouring the Moment?

In theory, it makes complete sense to enjoy the moment. Unfortunately, we live in a world where we've forgotten how to do this. We're the victims of our own success. From Emily Pankhurst to Margaret Thatcher and Condoleezza Rice, pioneering ladies around our planet have paved the way to a world of opportunity for us. Increasing equality in education and the workplace has cracked open a veritable treasure-chest of goodies for us to enjoy. The world really is a woman's oyster. But like oysters, too much of a good thing can sometimes leave you feeling sick.

Our lives have become like an 'eat all you can' buffet. Faced with the choice of anything you could possibly want, some of us have piled our plates far too high. Like frogs, our eyes are bigger than our tummies. Instead of enjoying gourmet meals, we end up with odd combinations of food that give us indigestion. And just as gluttony will keep you from heaven, there are seven deadly sins of time management which will keep you from enjoying and savouring every moment you have.

The Seven Deadly Sins of Time Management

Here they are, named and shamed, the sins that keep you from savouring your time.

Sin One: Impatience

Your lack of ability to keep your mind on one thing stops you from enjoying what you're doing. Your brain is always racing on to the next thing. You can't sit still and relax.

Sin Two: Guilt

Instead of enjoying what you're doing, you're busy beating yourself up about something else you think you should be doing instead.

Sin Three: Knowing No Boundaries

You're wound up like a spring. You find it difficult to relax into whatever you're up to at any given moment. You find it hard to switch from one thing to another. A classic example is the inability to fully make the transition from businesswoman to mum and mum to businesswoman.

Sin Four: Bad Language

You're always telling yourself that you're really busy and have no time. This bad language reinforces your belief that you're time-poor. It becomes a self-fulfilling prophecy.

Sin Five: Gluttony (Always Saying 'Yes' to More)

You don't know how to say 'No'. You often end up with so much on your plate you can't cope with it all. With too much, piled too high, you find it hard to focus on or enjoy any of it.

Sin Six: Treadmilling

You're on an uphill treadmill. You do the same old things day in, day out. Everything rolls into one. The mundane nature of your daily routine makes it difficult for you to engage with it in a satisfying way.

Sin Seven: Lust

You have a roving eye. You are constantly distracted and so you can't savour the moment.

Luckily, I've got a few sin solutions up my sleeve. And they're a lot easier than going on a diet!

Solution Number	1. Feel Present	2. Anchor Presence	3. Relaxation & Meditation	4. Guilt Be Gone	5. Ready, Steady, Focus	6. Boundary Management	7. Mental Markers	8. Good Language	9. The Shower of Power	10. Just Say No	11. Tame Your To-do Demon	12. Punctuate Time with Golden Events	13. Remove Distractions	14. Buffer Time
1. Impatience	X	X	X		X			X	X		X		X	X
2. Guilt				X										
3. Knowing No Boundaries	X	X	X			X	X							
4. Bad Language								X	X					
5. Gluttony										X				
6. Treadmilling												X		X
7. Lust			X		X							X	X	

Simple Sin Solutions

Solution One: Feel Present

Remember in Week Six when you drew your Time Line? Your Time Line provides you with a representation of how you see yourself in relation to your past, your present and your future.

It's a fabulous tool for helping you understand how well you savour the moment. Think back to your Time Line. Stand up and put yourself in the place that represents your present. How do you feel as you stand there? What do you see and what do you hear? Now, I know these may seem like rather bizarre questions, but stick with me. I promise it'll be worth it.

If you had to describe a representation of your present, what would you say about it? Let me give you some examples so you get the gist of what I'm talking about. I know when I first thought about how I perceived my present and I had to describe it to somebody, this is what I came up with.

I felt like I was standing on time. My present was tightly wrapped around me. So much so that it felt as if I was wearing a tight rubber suit that constrained me. I felt like I was trapped in the moment, which made it hard for me to enjoy it.

Here are some ways that other mums have told me they experience their present:

From the Mouths of Mums:

'I feel like a great big football being kicked at a goal. I think the goal in the distance represents the end of my life. My present is represented by the football. This football is rushing towards the goal too fast. I feel like there's a lot of momentum and I can't slow down. I want to slow

down, but it's like I'm flying through the air. That's what happens when you have three boys, I've been reduced to feeling like a football on the end of a muddy boot.'

'I feel like my present is all around me, like a big Christmas tree bauble. I've got plenty of space in here and it feels really comfortable.'

'I think a really good metaphor to describe the way I see my present is like an express train, one of those bullet ones you see in France and Germany. The ones that go so fast they're all blurry.'

'My present feels like a circular washing line, spinning round and round in the wind. I can't see the future or the past because I'm spinning so quickly. There's a load of tangled washing on the line. It's flapping in my face and I can't see anything else but that.'

What does your present feel like? If you had to describe it to someone else, what would you say? If you could think of a symbol or a metaphor to describe it, what would it be?

When you know, begin to wonder how useful is it in helping you enjoy the moment? For me, being constrained by a metaphorical rubber suit wasn't helpful. So I decided to start thinking about my present in a more constructive way. I began by imagining that in my present there was some space around me. I let the rubber hit the road and imagined I was wearing loose-fitting clothes. This alone gave me a different feeling about the present moment I found myself in. I also wanted to lose the feeling of being in a rush. I borrowed the idea of the Christmas bauble. What would it be like if I imagined I was in a bauble? Again it made me feel quite different, much more relaxed and evenly paced. Try imagining your present in some different ways that might help you enjoy what you're doing more.

If you're at work and you want to get things done quickly, it might be helpful to feel like an express train. When you're at home with your children, maybe it would be better to feel like a rowing boat. The poor woman who felt like a spinning washing line wasn't able to savour time at all when I first met her. We did some work on stopping her metaphorical washing line so it wasn't spinning any more. In her imagination she untangled all the washing, unpegged it and put it in a washing basket. She placed the basket behind her. She mentally unthreaded all the line from the whirligig and laid it out in a straight line. She then stood on the line. With the washing behind her and no spinning line in her present, she felt quite differently. She was able to look out into her future. That was something she'd not been able to do for a very long time.

Start to notice what your state is at any given moment. Think to yourself, what symbol would better serve me right now if I wanted to savour the moment more? Then choose to focus on feeling like that.

Solution Two: Anchor Presence

From the Mouths of Mums:

'Sometimes when I'm in a meeting at work I'll find I've switched off completely to what's being said and I'm thinking about what to make for supper. That's fine until someone asks me a question.'

Imagine if you had a built-in switch so that whenever you wanted to feel present to what you were doing you could. Just like flicking on a lightbulb you could have a feeling of presence at your fingertips. Using this Sin Solution, you can do just that. It works because it gives you a choice about how you feel.

Remember back in Week One we said time management is about *choice* and *focus*. You can choose to focus on feeling present and savouring your time or you can choose to focus on feeling hurried and manic. The useful thing about this exercise is it makes you think about how you are choosing to be. It empowers you to make a choice. We often feel like victims to our feelings, believing them to be controlled by external circumstances over which we have no influence. If you only have one choice about how you feel, then it's true you don't have any control. Give yourself another option. Learn how to feel present and then choose to feel that way. Here's how:

1. Think of a situation where you don't feel totally present, but would like to.
2. Decide how you would like to feel instead. For example, perhaps you would like to feel calm and engaged.
3. Recall a time from your past when you really felt that way.
4. As vividly as you can, as you recall a time when you had the desired feeling, take in all the *sounds*, all the *sights* and all the *feelings* from that memory. Concentrate on experiencing this as intensely as you can. (It might help to close your eyes.)
5. Stop concentrating and shake yourself gently, just to break the feeling.
6. Think about something you could use to trigger this positive feeling. An example might be clenching your fist, or putting your thumb and forefinger together.
7. Repeat Step four and relive the desired feeling as intensely as you can. Do this ten times.
8. When the feeling seems at its most intense, 'fire' the trigger you thought of in Step Six.
9. Stop concentrating on the memory. Shake yourself gently to break the feeling.
10. Test to see if the trigger works by recalling the situation where you lacked presence, identified in Step One. As you think about it, 'fire' your trigger. It should switch you into the positive feeling instantly. If not, repeat Steps Seven to Ten.

Try out your trigger in a situation whenever you feel yourself lacking total engagement. Notice how much more present you feel.

Solution Three: Relaxation and Meditation

Taking a few moments out every now and again really helps to ground you. If you regularly practise meditation or some form of relaxation, you will learn how to become more focused on and engaged in what you are doing. 'Little and often' is the motto once again. I'm a great fan of TM (transcendental meditation). My husband persuaded me to learn how to do this about 15 years ago. Initially I was a little cynical, thinking it might be a bit 'weirdy beardy' for my pragmatic tastes. To humour him I went along. To my surprise I found it very useful in helping me relax and tap into a state of presence whenever I wanted it. The TM Centre recommends meditating for 20 minutes, twice a day. Finding time to do this was a stretch even without children!

I remember in my group there was a woman who had a new baby. She complained that she never had time to meditate. 'She must be pretty incapable' I remember thinking to myself (I now have great respect that she actually made it to the meeting!). If you've got toddlers I recognize that it is sometimes difficult to get quiet time, but be creative. When they're asleep, meditate, or relax for ten minutes. Instead of switching the telly on, take a few minutes just to be with yourself. When things are really desperate I lock myself in the loo and leave my husband to get on with it!

There are some fabulous relaxation, meditation and self-hypnosis tapes and CDs on the market. Some of them are quite short and will teach you how to get into a more tranquil state. Alternatively, try this little relaxation technique even if it's only for five minutes.

The Garden of Tranquillity

Find yourself somewhere quiet and comfortable where you will not be disturbed. In your imagination you are about to visit the most beautiful, relaxing and tranquil garden in the world.

Close your eyes and just let go. Let every part of your body relax, from your toes to the crown of your head. When you feel as relaxed as you can, let yourself become ten times more relaxed. In your mind's eye take yourself to your own Garden of Tranquillity. In this garden the weather is perfect. The sky is clear and blue. Feel the warmth from the golden sun on your every limb. Just notice the relaxing sounds you hear, the smells. As you sink deeper into what feels like the most comfortable chair you've ever sat in, be aware of the colours and landscape in this mystical garden. As you relax, your breathing becomes deeper and slower. Enjoy the wonderful moments that you spend in your garden, knowing that while you're here there's nothing to be done, other than relax. Spend as long as you want in your garden. Only when you are ready, gently come back to the moment, refreshed and raring to go.

Tip! *Practise saying 'No' in the mirror – then when you get asked to do something you really don't have time for, the word 'No' will roll easily off your tongue!*

Solution Four: Guilt Be Gone

How many of us carry this baby around with us all the time? Unlike a Mulberry handbag or a pair of Jimmy Choos, nobody really wants it weighing down their shoulders and feet. Guilt is a useless emotion. I know secretly we all enjoy wallowing in it, but it serves no useful purpose. The only thing it does is allow us to feel self-righteous as we punish ourselves with mental beatings about things we've chosen to do in the past.

Things that we think we shouldn't have done. I'm sure you know the kind of things I mean:

From the Mouths of Mums:

'Oh, I feel so guilty because I should be spending more time with the children.'

'Oh, I feel bad because I was late for the school play. I should have been on time.'

'Oh, I feel guilty because I spend 50 hours a week at work. I should make more time for my family.'

If you're 'shoulding' all over yourself, stop it right now. While you're thinking 'should have', 'could have' and 'would have', it's hard to be present. Your thoughts are somewhere else. That place is the past, with an event that has happened. You have no control over the past. Why waste time focusing on it?

Guilt, the Useless Emotion

Instead of running guilty conversations in your head, try something more productive. Don't waste time fuzzying your focus by justifying choices you've made in the past. Instead, think about how you can get more control by making better choices about the things that currently make you feel guilty. Feeling guilty won't give you more time. Be bold and committed about the choices you make, rather than feeling guilty about them.

From the Mouths of Mums:

'I used to feel guilty about not spending enough time with the children, but as a single mum for financial reasons I had to work, I had no choice. When I was at work I felt guilty about not being at home. When I was at home I felt guilty because I was thinking about work. Basically I was wallowing in my own guilt, trying to make myself feel better about the fact I was working. All it did, though, was make me feel bad. When I got to grips with the fact that you can choose to feel however you want to feel, I knew that guilt

was the wrong choice. It didn't help me to feel good, in fact it dragged me down. Instead of feeling guilty I decided that I had to take responsibility for my choice to work. I decided to feel proud of myself for providing for my family and I decided to feel happy about it. I took control and focused my energy on putting structures and systems in place so that I could have as much RQT with my children as possible.

Instead of telling myself I was doing the wrong thing and feeling bad about it, I took total responsibility for what I was doing and then focused on making my life the best I could. Without guilt dragging me down, I found it much easier to savour my time. It was like a weight had been lifted from my shoulders.'

Most of us feel guilty about something and that leaves us unable to enjoy fully whatever we're doing. The list is long: having a facial, leaving the twins in the crèche, feeding the family fast food, using the video as a babysitter, staying late at the office. I could go on. I've had the privilege of meeting some of the UK's most successful 'MumPreneurs'. With the responsibility of children and large companies to cope with, how do they deal with guilt? I recently had the pleasure of meeting Emma Harrison, mother of four and founder of the highly successful company A4e. She's been voted one of the UK's top-100 entrepreneurs by 'Management Today' and was winner of the 2003 Woman Entrepreneur of the Year Award.

When I asked her if she ever felt guilty about her work and/or family life, she replied, 'Absolutely.' In fact, at one point her guilt was so bad she decided to tackle it head-on. The result? She made a plan about how she wanted things to be, and made clear choices about how she wanted to be as a mum. Her plan involved outsourcing much of the routine – for example, her husband is in charge of the bedtimes. She made a conscious choice to spend less time travelling backwards and forwards to London from her home in the north of England, and she recognized that her gift to her children is her creativity and love of life. She chooses to make all the time she spends with her children magical.

By making a plan, taking ownership of it and implementing it you put yourself back in control and are better able to deal with guilt. This seems to be a common trait I find in people who are able to feel good about what they are doing rather than guilty. In essence it's all about where you direct your energy and emotion. Do you direct yours positively by taking ownership and responsibility for the choices you make, or do you use them up worrying and feeling guilty? If it's the latter, think about how you can get control and feel good about your situation rather than becoming a victim of it. Try this exercise if you need to get rid of guilt.

Exercise – Getting Rid of Guilt

- Think of one thing you do with your time that makes you feel guilty. The guilty feeling then prevents you from being totally engaged in what you're doing.

- Mentally take responsibility for the fact that you are choosing to undertake the activity.
- Ask yourself, 'How do I want to feel instead of guilty?'
- Choose to feel the way you would rather feel. Focus on feeling like that.
- What else can you do to get control of the situation you're in, so you no longer have a need to feel guilty? Think of three things that will put you in control:

  1. ______________________________
  2. ______________________________
  3. ______________________________

- When you lose the guilty feeling you will be able to feel more present and savour what you are doing.

Solution Five: Ready, Steady, Focus

Sometimes just setting intent to focus can be really helpful. For instance, some mums find it hard to engage fully with a six-month-old, as they play peek-a-boo. Think about setting intent before the activity begins, to be fully present and to savour it. Challenge yourself to be present for just five minutes to start off with. Reward yourself when you succeed. Keep your focus in the present moment by really noticing what's around you. Notice the baby's bib, the chair he's sitting in, the coffee cup in your hand. All things that keep your mind held in the moment. Gradually, keep increasing the length of time you feel focused for. Like a muscle, exercise your focus span. It will get bigger and better.

Tip! *Don't waste time regretting things that have gone wrong.*

From the Mouths of Mums:

'Sometimes when I was reading a story to my daughter I was aware that I was rushing through it. I'd even miss pages out hoping she wouldn't notice. I just wanted to get to the end as quickly as possible and move on to the next thing. Anyway, I decided to make an effort to focus. I really took time to notice her expressions while I was reading and I decided to read the story like I was the most entertaining person in the world. I can't tell you what a difference it made to my enjoyment of reading the story, and I'm sure it made a big difference to her. She must have been able to tell I wasn't properly engaged before.'

Solution Six: Boundary Management

If you find that activities from different parts of your life seem to impinge on each other, making it hard for you to concentrate on only one of them, it might be helpful to put some boundaries in place. A really common issue for working mums is not switching off from work when they get home. For those mums who work from home this is even more of a challenge. If your office is on your kitchen table, is it surprising you think about work when you're making pudding? Decide what boundaries you want to set.

From the Mouths of Mums:

'I used to be really terrible at just nipping onto the computer at home when I got in from work. I used the excuse that I had overseas clients and they might be trying to contact me. A quick little peek at who had sent mail (overseas or otherwise) kept me at my computer all evening. Of course, I then felt guilty. In the end I made a deal with myself that I wouldn't go on the computer after 8pm. I fitted a plug with a timer so it wouldn't come on! Drastic times require drastic measures.'

'I run my own curtain-making business from home and one of my bedrooms is a sewing room. I had a lock fitted and made myself lock up at the end of the day, just like I would if I was in a curtain workshop. It also kept the kids off the fabrics!'

Solution Seven: Mental Markers

If you find it hard to separate out activities, think of some 'mental markers' that will make it easier for you to switch from one to the other. That way you can be fully 'in' whichever one you're undertaking. For example, when you leave the office at night, the revolving door could be your first mental marker.

That door means you're leaving work. When you walk through your front door, use that door as a marker to remind you that you are home. As you step into the house, mentally recalibrate to 'home mode'. Change into a different set of clothes. Have different mental markers and triggers that tell you you are focusing on a particular part of your life at that moment in time.

From the Mouths of Mums:

'The first thing I do now when I get home is change out of my suit. I wouldn't go to the office in my pyjamas and breastfeed the baby, so why should I walk around the house in my work clothes? What I'm wearing helps me make a mental separation between work and home. I try not to relive my work day by talking about it too much. I just get straight into being Mum, and focusing on that. My kids don't care about the office politics.'

Solution Eight: Good Language

The language we use can have a profound effect on the way we feel. Do you often tell others that you have no time? You don't know where the time goes? Or you won't have time to do that today? Using this type of language, as you now know, sets an internal expectation that this will be the case. Think about all the things you say that could send you into a spin and contribute to you not feeling present, simply because you've told yourself that you have so much on, you don't have time to be present. You're mentally in a rush.

Here are some great examples of language that can make you feel rushed:

- I just haven't got time.
- I can't believe the holidays have gone already.
- I just don't know where the time went.
- I rush from one place to the next.
- I've just got too much to do.
- I never have a minute to myself.
- My body aches and needs help.
- We got there by the skin of our teeth.
- I just run from one thing to the next.
- I meet myself on the way out of the door when I'm coming in.
- Where are the years going?
- I feel trapped by time, there's no way out.
- I never stand still.
- I spend all day wishing for the end of the day when the kids are in bed.
- I'm really looking forward to the next stage of my child's development.

How much of this type of bad language is polluting your brain? Make a mental note each time you use a phrase that tells you you're hurried. Then say the phrase again, this time preceding it with the words 'It used to be that ...' Follow it with the words '... but I'm not like that any more.'

For example, if you catch yourself saying, 'I rush from one place to the next,' change it to *'It used to be that* I rushed from one place to the next, *but I'm not like that any more.'*

Solution Nine: The Shower of Power

Throw out the old language and bring in the new. How about dreaming up some useful, positive statements to add to your vocabulary? Vocabulary that will help you feel present and unrushed. Often known as positive affirmations, these will put you in a marvellous mental state, leaving you more open to being present. Here's an affirmation that one of my clients came up with:

From the Mouths of Mums:

'I am calm and focused. I am present to all the activities that I choose to do. I know there is enough time to get everything done, in an orderly way.'

Affirmations are a statement of how you would like to be, but written in the present tense and positive in nature.

Here are a few more:

From the Mouths of Mums:

'I always arrive where I'm going on time.'
'I know how to enjoy every moment.'
'My time passes at just the pace I want it to.'

What could you be saying to yourself that would help you feel more present? Think of one affirmation that would override any negative affirmations you're carrying around in your head. Some motivational gurus advocate an 'hour of power' in the morning, when you focus on your affirmations and mental preparation for the day. I say get real, we're mums. Instead, I advocate the 'Shower of Power'. While you're douching your delectables, get your mental matter mustered and mutter your affirmations. What a great way to start the day.

Tip! *Buy insurance for plumbing, heating, wiring, etc. so you have 24-hour cover 365 days a year.*

Solution Ten: Just Say No

Do you often find yourself saying 'Yes' when you should be saying 'No'? Are you constantly biting off more than your canines can comfortably chew? We've all done it – agreeing to help with the school disco, going for a coffee with someone you barely know, telling the children you'll take them swimming when you've got a report to write. You then find you've taken on too much and can't focus on anything properly.

We say 'Yes' for all sorts of reasons. We don't want to disappoint, we want to appear helpful and we don't want to look like we can't cope. Beware, people who can't say 'No' have a tendency to drown in a pool of their own self-generated to-dos.

What kinds of things are you saying 'Yes please' to when you'd rather be saying 'No thank you'? Think of three recent things:

1. ____
2. ____
3. ____

List three situations that are likely to come up in the near future where you know you will want to say 'No':

1. ____
2. ____
3. ____

How will you deal with these situations when they arise?

Tip! *Lift-share wherever possible for the school run, after-school clubs or other activities.*

The Keys to Setting a 'No' Free

Having the courage to say 'No' isn't always easy. However, it is possible to say 'No' in way that gets us off the hook, without appearing uncooperative or rude. Here are some keys to setting a 'No' free:

1. *Engage your brain.*

   Think before you speak. Sometimes we blurt out a 'Yes' before we've even really thought about it. Don't be afraid to say, 'Can I let you know?' or 'I need to think about it.' This is particularly good if you're the kind of person who needs to work up to saying 'No'.

2. *Put your sanity first.*

   Often we say 'Yes' instead of 'No' because we don't want to upset people. We want to please all of the people all of the time. We're fabulous at keeping everyone happy except ourselves. Do you need to please all of the people? If you're being asked to do something that you really don't want to do, like listen to a telesales call, just say 'No'. Don't those calls always happen at teatime, or is that just me? Practise saying 'No' to yourself in the mirror. That way, when it comes to the real thing you'll be well practised in how to do it.

   Think about the consequences of your actions. Ask yourself the 'What if?' question. 'What will happen if I say yes?' and 'What will happen if I say no?' Will your life, or the life of the person making the request of you, grind to a halt if you say 'No'? If you start feeling guilty, please go straight to Sin Solution Number Four.

3. *Yes but not yet.*

   Sometimes we have to do things we'd rather not. I'm thinking particularly of work. When you've got childcare and the boss asks you to do a 30-minute job 20 minutes before you're meant to leave, how do you say 'No' without seeming unreasonable? I suggest you use the 'Yes but not yet' technique. What this means is that you're willing to say 'Yes' but not at this exact moment. A response to this request might be:

- Yes I can do it by tomorrow lunchtime, is that OK?
- Yes I can start it now and complete it tomorrow.
- Yes I can do it. When is the latest I can give it to you?
- Yes I can do it, but is it more important than what I'm doing, because if I do this then I won't be able to do that. What's the priority, what do you want me to do first?

  By taking this approach you show willing and that you're not to be dumped on at the last minute. The more you let people dump on you, the more they will happily dump.

  If you use this technique with your children, make sure you keep your promises. If you commit to deliver at a certain time, do it. They will learn that you mean what you say. So often we say we'll do it later and then we don't.

4. *I'd like to, but I can't.*

   Empathize, be assertive not aggressive. 'No' doesn't have to be nasty. Explain why you can't do it:

   'I'd love to help out, but we've got family commitments that weekend. Perhaps I can help next time.'

5. *No I can't, but I know a man who can.*

   Is there someone else who can help with this request? If so, point them in the right direction. Be as helpful as you can. Even though you are saying 'No' to the request, what else could you do to help them?

6. *No, I can't do that – but I can do …*

   Is there something else you can do instead to help this person? 'I can't help with the organization of the dance, but I'll sell some raffle tickets for you.'

   When you show people that you respect your time by saying 'No', they begin to respect it too. The more we say 'Yes' the more people expect from us. We end up running ourselves into the ground and feeling resentful (another useless emotion).

   Remember, you have control over the choice you make when you say 'Yes' or 'No'. Who's more important, the person you're saying 'Yes' to, or you? By using the techniques above, you give others more choices, too. This makes it easier for you to say 'No' without slamming the door in their face.

Solution 11: Tame Your To-do Demon

Do you have a voice in your head constantly nagging you about what you need to do next? I do, and I call it Wilma What's Next.

She reminds me what I have to do next when I'm in the middle of what I'm doing. She doesn't want me to forget my schedule. This prevents me from being able to completely savour what I'm doing. She thinks she's helping me. I think she's nagging. Into the bargain, now I've got fabulous systems and planning tools, I don't need reminding. I'm confident that things will happen when they should, without her pestering me. She's like a record running in my head. How on earth do you get rid of it?

Acknowledge your voice and recognize that, like the rest of your Management Team, it's trying to help you. You might think that it's nagging, but in reality it's trying to ensure that you get everything done and don't forget things.

Reassure your Wilma What's Next that you now have a wonderful planning system which allows you to capture all that has to be done and everything is under control.

Respectfully ask her to be quiet while you savour what you are doing. Reassure her that you will check with her when you are unsure about what's next. If she still speaks, use the volume-control knob in your head, like we did in Week Six. Turn down the volume until the voice is no longer audible.

Tip! *Don't bring work home.*

Solution 12: Punctuate Time with Golden Events

As we get older, time seems to go faster and faster. Often events blur into one another and we struggle to remember what on earth we've been up to. Have you ever had the experience of calling a friend you've not spoken to for a while? Your first question is, 'What have you been up to?' and her reply is, 'Oh, just the usual, not much' or 'I've been really busy, but I can't remember what on earth I've been doing.' It's hard, isn't it, to look back and savour memories that you can't recall? If everything is rolling into one, you need to think about how you can punctuate your Time Line with significant events, not just routine stuff.

When you're in it, routine can seem to drag. When you look back it seems to have gone quickly. Often it's because there's not much to separate one day from the next in your memory. If you can manage to create routine for the humdrum things, you'll have loads of time left over for interesting pursuits. By creating memorable events that punctuate your Time Line, you can separate one chunk of time from another. There's spontaneity and excitement breaking up the routine events.

When we're younger, time seems to go really slowly. Your life is full of new and exciting memories: your first day at school, your first kiss, your wedding and your first baby are all big, memorable events. They help us remember that part of our life. As we get older (sorry to mention it), big events that naturally punctuate our Time Line get a bit thin on the ground. Unless of course you count divorces!

So, why not make your own 'golden events'? This way, when you look back you've got some golden memories to punctuate your life. Things to think about might be creating your own family traditions. Take time to savour the planning of holidays. At the beginning of a year ask, 'What can we do as a family, or as individuals, that will help this year stand out?'

Most people don't have their family photos or video footage sorted in any meaningful way. Have a family evening sorting out photos. What a wonderful way to savour what you've been up to! As I write this, it's January. My family and I have sat down to plan all the fun things we'd like to do this year. A suggestion from my eight-year-old son was a trip to Paris on Eurostar. I'm looking forward to it already. For us it will be a family first. Start spicing up your Time Line. Your life will look less like a tangled bowl of spaghetti and more like a long string of brightly coloured bunting.

Tip! *Clear your fridge of old food every other day before it becomes a permanent fixture.*

Solution 13: Remove Distractions

Short of shooting your children, it's hard to imagine how you could remove all distractions from your life so you can completely focus on what you're doing. I know sometimes when I work with mums on planning they'll say to me, 'How can I possibly focus on my plan? I know that before I've managed to pick up my pen to cross off A1, I'll be interrupted. Somebody will disturb me. The phone will ring, Olivia will put pink nail varnish on my bathroom floor and the cat will be sick on the carpet. There's no way I'll be able to work undisturbed through my list, and just savour what I'm doing. It's never going to happen.'

It's a common problem. In a recent study at the University of California, some interesting statistics were discovered about distractions. It was noted that a group of information workers spent on average about three minutes on a task before being interrupted to do something else. Distractions are a fact of life at home and at work. The question is, how do we deal with these interruptions and distractions so we can focus? Here are a few suggestions for removing them:

- *Excuse me, who's interrupting you?*

  Be aware that many of the interruptions we encounter in a typical day are self-inflicted. Notice which ones you're in control of and which ones you're not. Get rid of the ones you can control.

- *Children*

  One of the biggest complaints from mums is that they can't focus because their children are always around. This is particularly true if you've got pre-school children. If you want focus time without them distracting you, think about all your options for childcare. If you can build in some regular spots during the week when you know you won't be disturbed, it can make the world of difference. How about giving your other half, granny or a friend a regular time-slot with the children? Give other family members some RQT with the children so you can have some RQT with yourself. You know what they say: 'Absence makes the heart grow fonder.' Having these regular breaks from the children allows you to appreciate them when they come back. With older children you can ask them to wait, as you would if you were at work. Tell them that you will be free in five minutes or ten minutes. Be sure to follow through. You can even ask them to come back and remind you in five minutes. If you consistently do what you say, you will find children can be quite accommodating.

- *Phone calls*

  Please use the answer machine and screen your calls. Only answer if it's convenient. When you call other people back, tell them how long you've got to spend on the phone with them. If it's two minutes, make it two minutes.

- *Get rid of items that distract you*

  Do you have a compulsion to look at the photos in the album by the side of the sofa every time you walk past? Do you pick up a magazine you've read 100 times already? If something constantly physically distracts you, put it away. Start to really notice what it is that distracts you. When you have this awareness you can begin to work out a plan to remove it.

- *Ask people not to distract you*

  A bit obvious, I know, but tell people when you need quiet time. Ask them not to call round or phone then.

Tip! *Only iron what you really have to – ask yourself, 'When I'm on my death bed, will I be glad I spent ten minutes of my life ironing this particular garment?'*

Solution 14: Buffer Time

If you find that you can't focus because you feel rushed, start planning in buffer time. How long did you think a minute lasted? Do you have a realistic grasp of time? If not, start to notice how long things really take. If you get your estimates right, it avoids the need to be rushing on to the next thing. Schedule lots of buffer time into your day, so that emergencies can be dealt with. Let's face it, we know things will happen that we haven't planned on. It's a fact of life.

Give yourself some contingency. When you're planning, add on up to 20 per cent more time than you think a task will take. Aim to arrive somewhere five minutes earlier than you need to. Do your most valuable activities first. You'll feel more present and in control, just by giving yourself a little bit more space to breathe and focus.

Absolution

So there you have it, sin solutions to all seven Time-Management Sins. Use the sin solutions and you'll find out what it is to live in the moment and savour every magical minute of every marvellous day. You have the tools, you have the techniques, you have the power of choice. Like the hare and the tortoise, the mum who paces herself will get more done, enjoy it more and arrive at the finishing line in a better state. The mum who approaches life like it's a 100-yard dash, well, as we all know, she experiences life quite differently. If you're not enjoying the moment, ask yourself what you have to change about how you're being to make a difference. When you have the answer, just do it. Each moment of your life creates your future, so make each one of them magical and create the future you desire, deserve and dream of.

A Final Thought: Whom Are You Becoming?

There was once a woman who lived by a lake. At the end of each day, as the sun was setting, she would go for a walk by the still water. As she strolled through the grass she felt the warmth of the setting sun on her face, as she listened to the birds sing. Each evening as she neared the end of her walk she picked up a pebble and threw it into the lake. 'Another day gone,' she'd say to herself as the pebble hit the water. But even though the pebble had disappeared, the ripples it made on the surface were still there, long after the pebble had sunk to the bottom of the lake, never to be seen again. As she watched the concentric circles, she asked herself the same three questions she'd asked every evening since she'd become a mother:

1. What did I do today that was important to me?
2. How did I savour today?
3. What did I do today that will make positive ripples in my future?

She quietly took a moment to answer these questions. Then, when she was ready, she walked back towards her home, where her children, grandchildren, great-grandchildren and many friends were eagerly awaiting their favourite person to celebrate her 90th birthday.

What future is your present creating for you? The choice is yours.

Tip! *Are your children doing too many after-school activities? Are you all overscheduled?*

Actions for Week Seven

- Buy a box of chocolates. Each day, eat one chocolate. Make it last as long as you can. Really focus on it. Notice its texture, its taste, the smell, any sounds that it makes as you eat it. How do you feel as you savour it? Notice what it's like when you totally focus on savouring something.
- Every day for the next seven days, choose two activities that you will totally focus on and be totally present for.
- Notice when you are not savouring the moment. Ask yourself, 'What's stopping me from savouring what I'm doing?'
- When you have the answer, work out what you have to do to regain focus. Use a sin solution.
- Each night for the rest of your life, before you go to bed, ask yourself:

1. What did I do today that was important to me?
2. How did I savour today?
3. What did I do today that will make positive ripples in my future?

- Make a promise to yourself, that tomorrow, and every day for the rest of your life, you will choose to focus on what is most valuable to you in your life.

Tip! *Have a running shopping list, easily accessible to everyone.*

Summary

- To be or not to be? This is the question. Many of us are so busy doing we've forgotten how to just be.
- How you relate to time will affect your ability to savour it.
- There are Seven Sins in Time Management that will prevent you from savouring the moment: Impatience, Guilt, Knowing No Boundaries, Bad Language, Gluttony, Treadmilling and Lust.
- Each sin has a number of solutions that will absolve you, thus allowing you to savour the moment.

Tip! *The wastepaper bin is the most time-efficient filing system there is.*

What's Next?

As you enter Week Eight, you have all the tools you need to get everything done and live the life of your dreams. Not bad in less than two months. All you have to do now is keep up these new good habits. Always keep the Seven Truths of Time Management close to you. Remember, 'the truth will set you free.' When things don't seem quite right in your life, ask yourself, 'which one of the Seven Truths am I violating?' Then, work to get back on track.

Over the past seven weeks you will have noticed that when you take charge of your world, it changes. When you take responsibility and empower yourself to do something different, you get different results. You get control. So, what's next? Well, keep up the good work. Keep implementing what you've learned. Now you're the most organized person in the world, people will want to know your secret. Tell them how it's done. Most important of all, teach this magic to your children. Give them the gift of managing their own time. It will change their lives, too. As Ralph Waldo Emerson said:

'Sow a thought and you reap an action; sow an act and you reap a habit; sow a habit and you reap a character; sow a character and you reap a destiny.'

Continue to sow the seeds of learning you've found in this book. As you leave manic behind and embrace marvellous, reach for the stars and reap the destiny of your dreams. You're a mum, you're marvellous and you deserve it.

The End
Or just the beginning ...?

Afterword

Dear Allison,

What can I say? It worked! Seven weeks on and I'm a changed woman. Never in my wildest dreams did I think it would be possible to tame my tragic time-management ways.

Just to give you an idea of how different things really are, here's a snapshot of my day today (a Saturday). I'm sure you'll agree it's quite different from the last one I shared with you! I woke up half an hour early feeling energetic and looking forward to the day ahead. After my shower of power, I prepared breakfast for the whole family. This is now part of our weekly family routine. We actually ate together and made pleasant conversation. A little outrageous outsourcing meant my husband and children cleared up while I quickly picked out the swimming bags from their new home (a hook by the back door), got my aerobics gear on and put out a frozen casserole to thaw and later heat up for lunch.

The children have a bit of 'RQT' with Dad in the local pool on a Saturday morning now while I do a gym class. Yes, with my new rolling menu and internet shopping list my Saturday morning supermarket shuffle is a thing of the past, and I now bring some 'me time' into my near focus. After my class I met up with the children and husband in town for a milkshake and cappuccino en famille. Returned my library book on time, and chose some new ones with the children.

When we got home I sat down to do spelling homework x 3. The reward for completing this: a game of scrabble and some time looking at the new library books. At 3.00 my mobile-phone calendar rang to remind me to take the girls to their party. I was able to find the invitation, directions and previously wrapped gift immediately. While they were out I put together the final bits and pieces for my dinner party, which I have to say is the simplest but most tasty supper you'll ever come across. With two guests bringing pudding and another the starter, it's been no trouble preparing this and for once I was feeling really relaxed about entertaining eight people.

At 7.45 with the youngest in bed and the eldest happily watching a DVD, my friends arrived for dinner to a clean house, a hostess with the mostest who was ready for action – and wearing earrings and lipstick that actually matched! We had a great giggle over a jug of wine (apples and blueberries removed) and no one can quite believe that I, tamed Manic Mum, could have done all this in one day and still seem calm and relaxed.

With the guests gone I persuaded my husband to help clear up the debris in a way that only a woman who's lost 10 pounds and feels like a sex kitten can!

My 'Daily Dozen' planning minutes done, I know that tomorrow I'll be having a guilt-free lie-in. Since I delegated rifling through my receipt box in an attempt to sort out my accounts to my accountant, my Sundays have become my own again.

This, Allison, is just the tip of the iceberg. My life really has changed, I feel differently about myself and other people treat me differently. I'm focusing on the things I really want to do. Life just seems better. It's hard to believe that such small changes can bring about such big results, but they have. I send you my gratitude for helping me change my life of manic mundaneness to one of organized joy.

Thankfully

A Marvellous Mum

Notes

Notes

Notes

Notes

Notes

Titles of Related Interest

Feel Happy Now
by Michael Neill

Cosmic Ordering for Beginners
by Barbel Mohr

Everything I've Ever Learned About Change
by Lesley Garner

How to Stop Your Kids Watching too Much TV
by Teresa Orange and Louise O'Flynn

What Are You Really Eating
by Amanda Ursell

Repotting
by Diana Holman and Ginger Pape

We hope you enjoyed this Hay House book.
If you would like to receive a free catalogue featuring additional Hay House books and products, or if you would like information about the Hay Foundation, please contact:

Hay House UK Ltd
292B Kensal Rd • London W10 5BE
Tel: (44) 20 8962 1230; Fax: (44) 20 8962 1239
www.hayhouse.co.uk

***

Published and distributed in the United States of America by:
Hay House, Inc. • PO Box 5100 • Carlsbad, CA 92018-5100
Tel.: (1) 760 431 7695 or (1) 800 654 5126;
Fax: (1) 760 431 6948 or (1) 800 650 5115
www.hayhouse.com

Published and distributed in Australia by:
Hay House Australia Ltd • 18/36 Ralph St • Alexandria NSW 2015
Tel.: (61) 2 9669 4299; Fax: (61) 2 9669 4144
www.hayhouse.com.au

Published and distributed in the Republic of South Africa by:
Hay House SA (Pty) Ltd • PO Box 990 • Witkoppen 2068
Tel./Fax: (27) 11 706 6612 • orders@psdprom.co.za

Published and distributed in India by:
Hay House Publishers India • Muskaan Complex • Plot No.3
B-2 • Vasant Kunj • New Delhi – 110 070.
Tel.: (91) 11 41761620; Fax: (91) 11 41761630.
contact@hayhouseindia.co.in

Distributed in Canada by:
Raincoast • 9050 Shaughnessy St • Vancouver, BC V6P 6E5
Tel.: (1) 604 323 7100; Fax: (1) 604 323 2600

***